# CLASSIC
# STEAM

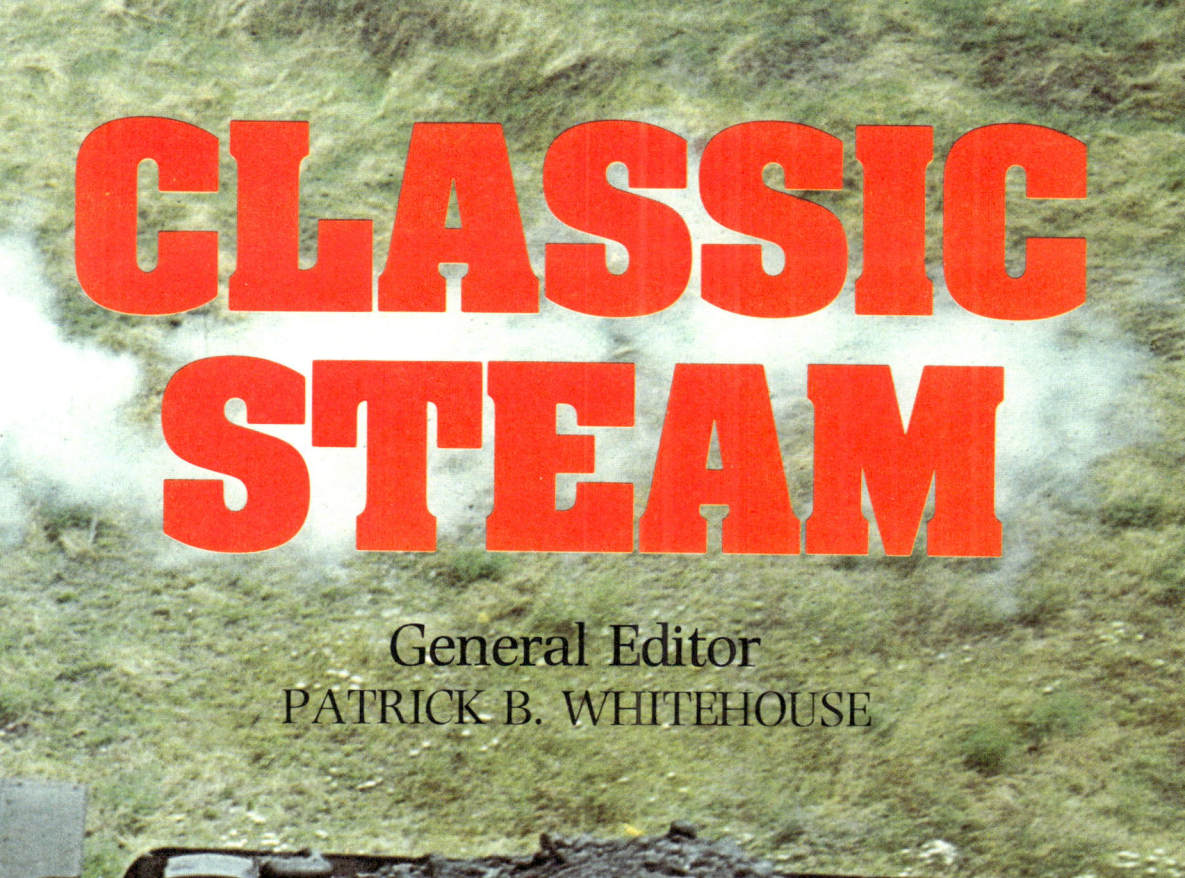

# CLASSIC STEAM

General Editor
PATRICK B. WHITEHOUSE

# HAMLYN

LONDON · NEW YORK · SYDNEY · TORONTO

 A BISON BOOK

Published by
Bison Books Limited
4 Cromwell Place
London SW7

© Copyright Bison Books Limited 1980

Distributed by
The Hamlyn Publishing Group Limited
London · New York · Sydney · Toronto
Astronaut House, Feltham
Middlesex, England

ISBN 600 34948 1

All rights reserved. No part of this publication may be reproduced,
stored in a retrieval system, or transmitted, in any form or by any
means, electronic, mechanical, photocopying, recording or otherwise,
without the permission of The Hamlyn Publishing Group Limited
and the copyrightholder.
First published 1980

Printed in Hong Kong

Produced by Colourviews Limited for Bison Books
under the direction of Patrick Whitehouse

Editorial Consultants: Martin Hedges, Basil Cooper
Designer: Adrian Hodgkins

General view of Waterloo
Station Southern Region
with an express for
Bournemouth hauled by
a Bulleid Pacific.

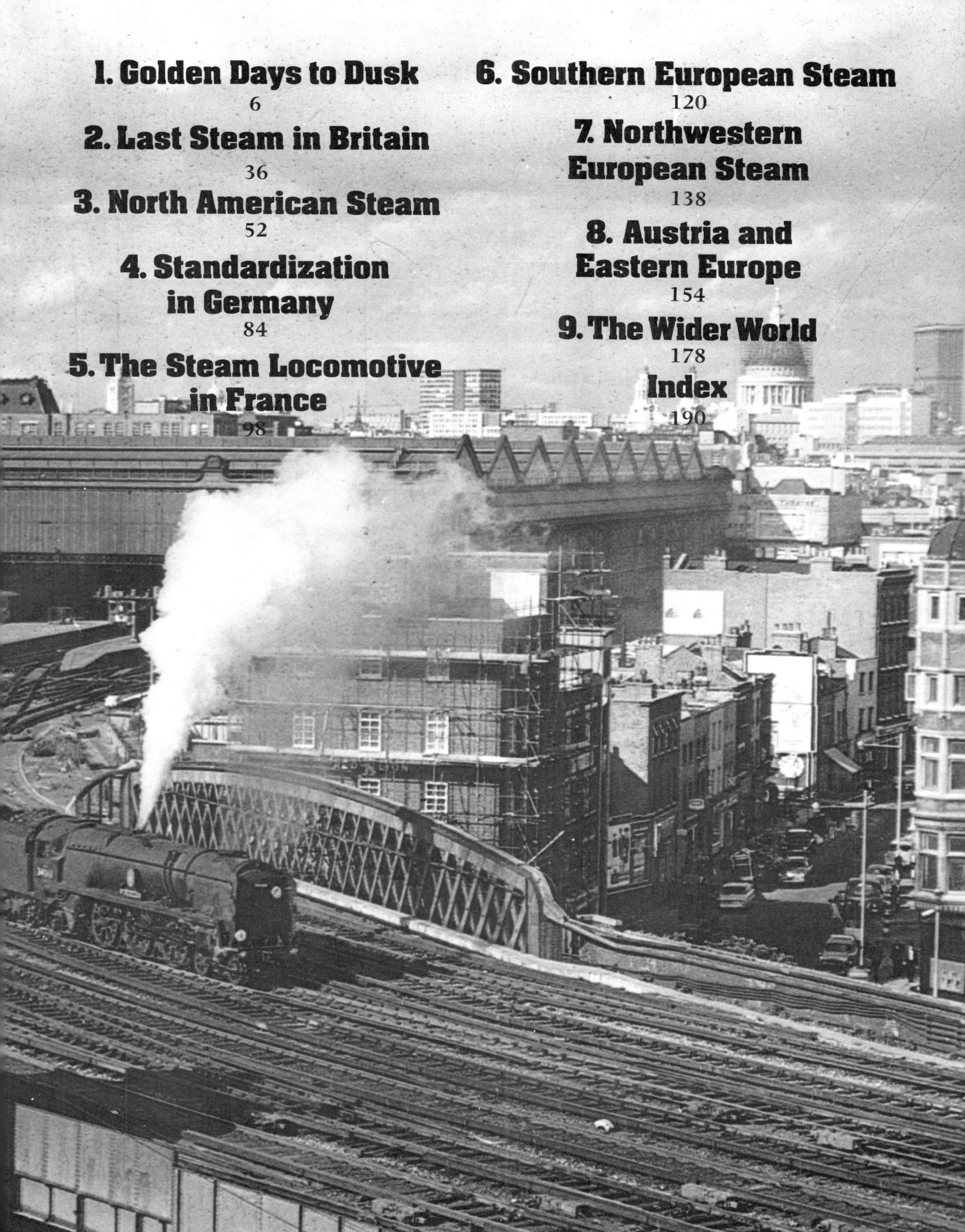

# 1. Golden Days to Dusk

As the birthplace of the steam railway, Britain has nourished a school of writers on the subject. The opening in 1825 of the Stockton & Darlington Railway was less than one lifetime away when E Foxwell and T C Farrer surveyed contemporary railway speed on a worldwide scale in their classic work *Express Trains English and Foreign*. The authors, writing in 1889, gave two definitions of an express. In Great Britain and the United States it was 'any train which attains a speed, including stops, of 40 miles an hour,' to which they added the condition that 'it must as a rule cover a distance of at least 40 miles.' In all other places their speed criterion was 29 mph (47 kph).

Some 40 years after Farrer and Foxwell, at the beginning of the 1930s, there had been a levelling up of speed throughout the world. The mile-a-minute average, start-to-stop, was being achieved and bettered but still on a fairly limited scale and often on short runs. In Great Britain a dramatic change occurred in 1932, giving full rein to the capabilities of five locomotive classes which had made their appearance a few years earlier and were destined to take their place among the giants of the steam age.

First, in chronological order, was H N Gresley's Pacific 4–6–2 design for the Great Northern Railway, which appeared in 1922 (a year before the 43 individual main-line railway companies in Great Britain were amalgamated into four groups and the Great Northern was merged into the London & North Eastern Railway). The only previous British Pacific had been *The Great Bear* on the Great Western Railway, but this locomotive had a restricted sphere of activity because of its weight and was subsequently reconstructed as a 4–6–0.

The second of the five classes was the Great Western 'Castle' class 4–6–0 designed by C B Collett and introduced in 1923. This was the year of the 'Grouping' previously mentioned, in which Great Western alone retained its title but absorbed many smaller companies which had long been closely identified with it operationally. Collett built on the foundation of the highly successful four-cylinder 'Star' class designed by his predecessor, G J Churchward, but enlarged the cylinder diameter from 15 to 16 inches (381 to 406 mm) and designed a new and larger boiler to supply steam. The result was a locomotive developing a tractive effort of 31,625 lb at 85 percent of the boiler pressure of 225 lb per square inch (15.8 kg/sq cm), overtopping the 29,835 lb of the heavier Gresley Pacific, which had a boiler pressure of 180 lb per square inch (12.6 kg/sq cm).

In 1924 the first 'Castle' – No 4073, *Caerphilly Castle* – and the first Gresley Pacific – No 4470, *Great Northern* – were on show in the Palace of Engineering at the British Empire Exhibition at Wembley near London. The Great Western Railway proclaimed its new product as 'the most powerful express passenger locomotive in Great Britain,' gaining considerable prestige in the eyes of the public in consequence. Gresley took up the challenge and invited the Great Western to substantiate its claim by a practical demon-

Above: LNER A3 Pacific No 4472, *Flying Scotsman*, as preserved at Carnforth Depot.

Far left: Ex-LMS Jubilee class 4—6—0 outside Holbeck shed, Leeds in 1967. This was the last year of regular service for this class and the locomotive, No 45593, *Kolhapur*, was used for parcels traffic together with the summer Saturday expresses to Scotland via the Settle–Carlisle main line of the one-time Midland Railway.

Left: Ex-Great Western Railway Castle class No 5027 at Carmarthen, South Wales.

Right: Sir Nigel Gresley's A3 class Pacific No 4472, *Flying Scotsman*, on the East Coast main line of the former LNER near Aycliffe, County Durham, in 1969, preserved by Alan Pegler.

stration. The GWR accepted, and in May 1925 the 'Castle' class locomotive No 4079, *Pendennis Castle* was sent to work on the London & North Eastern Railway main line between King's Cross and Doncaster, while LNER's Pacific No 4474, *Victor Wild*, took up duties on the Great Western main line between Paddington and Plymouth. At the end of the exchange the 'Castle' showed an average fuel consumption 3.7 lb per mile less than that of the Pacific when burning Yorkshire coal and 6 lb per mile less with its traditional fuel, Welsh coal, on its home ground. These results led Gresley to modify the valve gear of his Pacifics and later to rebuild one of them in 1927 with a 220 lb per square inch (15.5 kg/sq cm) boiler and larger superheater. From this there followed a second Pacific series with improved efficiency. It appeared in the early 1930s and served as the precursor of the developments in high speeds and long nonstop runs the decade was to bring.

One of the new companies created by the 'Grouping' of 1923 was the Southern Railway in which were incorporated the lines of the former South Eastern & Chatham Joint Committee connecting London with the Channel ports of Dover and Folkestone. The first express locomotive produced under the auspices of the new Southern Railway was R E L Maunsell's 'Lord Nelson' class 4—6—0, built specifically for the growing Continental holiday traffic, now calling for motive power able to work 500-ton trains at a start-to-stop average of 55 mph (89 kph). Maunsell's four-cylinder design had the novel feature

that the cranks on the two driving axles were set so that they were at 135 degrees to each other and there were eight exhaust beats per revolution. The grate area was no more than 33 square feet (306.6 square dm), the maximum possible with a narrow firebox.

On a paper calculation the 'Lord Nelsons' could produce a tractive effort of 33,500 lb (15,195 kg), outdoing the 'Castles' and the Gresley Pacifics in this respect, but as originally built the engines did not always steam well enough to sustain such an output. In later years their performance was improved by modifications to the blastpipe and chimney.

Whether actual or theoretical, the 'Lord Nelsons' lead in the power league was short-lived for in 1927 two more noteworthy classes appeared within a few weeks of each other, one of which — Great Western's 'King' — was rated at over 40,000 lb (18,144 kg) tractive effort, enough to give it a lead over its contemporaries with some allowance for the full calculated figure not being met. The 'King' class 4—6—0 was another Collett design and, like his 'Castle,' an extension of the principles in the Churchward 'Stars.' Boiler pressure in the 'King' was raised to 250 lb per square inch (17.6 kg/sq cm), the first time such a high pressure had been used in a British locomotive, and although both heating surface and grate area were less than in Gresley's improved Pacifics, the type of firebox favored by the Great Western design team had long proved itself capable of making the fuel burned in it yield maximum heat energy.

Above: The first British Pacific locomotive, Great Western No 111, *The Great Bear*, built to the design of G J Churchward in 1908, heads a Cheltenham tea-car express on the Paddington-Swindon portion of its journey.
Above left: After the first batch of Gresley Pacifics, a second series was built with higher boiler pressure. One of this later batch, No 2547, *Donovan*, heads the up 'Flying Scotsman' shortly after being fitted with a corridor tender for making the nonstop run between London and Edinburgh.
Left: LNER Pacific No 4472, *Flying Scotsman*, leaves King's Cross with the 'Flying Scotsman' express on its first nonstop run to Edinburgh on 1 May 1928. No 4472 was the second of Gresley's Pacifics, the first being No 4470, *Great Northern*. It is now preserved and in private ownership.

The 'Kings,' 'Castles,' Gresley Pacifics and Southern 'Lord Nelsons' were all recognizable as developments of what had gone before on their respective railways, particularly the 'Castles' and 'Kings' with their traditional Great Western copper-capped chimney, polished brass safety-valve casing, and polished brass beading over the splashers. The 'Kings' added another touch of color with the brass of their outside axleboxes for the leading bogie axle. This arrangement was necessary in order to provide independent springing for all wheels of the bogie. The springs for the leading wheels had to be outside the bogie frame in order to clear the inside cylinders, while those for the other pair of wheels were inside to be clear of the outside cylinders.

In contrast to the rest, the fifth of the big express passenger engines of the late 1920s was startlingly different from anything seen before on the main line from London Euston station to the north and Scotland. This was the 'Royal Scot' 4–6–0 of the London Midland & Scottish Railway, a design produced in some haste to fill a gap in that company's motive power resources.

The LMS authorities were interested in the performance of the GWR 'Castles' and in 1926 borrowed No 5000, *Launceston Castle*, for trials between Euston station, Crewe and Carlisle in the north. The results convinced them of the need for a new 4–6–0 conceived in the modern manner, but they had left things late considering the developments on the other lines. The design office was put urgently to work, and

Left: There was a short period during the end of the 1950s/early 1960s when British Rail paid considerable attention to liveries and smartness. Here, at Newcastle, BR 0–6–0T No 68723 shunts resplendent in North Eastern Railway green.

Right: Ex-Great Western Railway No 6960, *Raveningham Hall,* as preserved on the Severn Valley Railway at Bridgnorth.

Below: An unknown GWR 'Castle' heads a down express out of Box Tunnel on the main line to Bristol during the early days of British Rail.

Bottom: LNER A4 class Pacific No 4498, *Sir Nigel Gresley,* at Carnforth Depot.

the Southern Railway collaborated by loaning drawings of its 'Lord Nelson' class. Certain constructional features were copied from this source, but the major influences on the design of the new LMS 4–6–0 were those aspects of the Great Western 'Castle' which made it so effective in the generation and use of steam, as demonstrated by *Launceston Castle* in the trials. The contract for production was put out to the North British Locomotive Company Limited and by the autumn of 1927 the first 'Scots' were reaching the LMS. Tractive effort for this three-cylinder locomotive was 33,150 lb (15,036.6 kg) and the boiler pressure 250 lb per square inch (17.6 kg/sq cm). It was an impressive locomotive but distinctive rather than handsome, its appearance spoiled by a very small chimney perched on a very large-diameter smokebox. The boiler was similarly rotund, and the top of the firebox sloped down toward the cab to help in accommodating the whistle within the loading gauge; even then it had to be mounted horizontally.

In this busy period of new locomotive types, many important services were still being worked by locomotives of various wheel arrangements, built by the pre-'Grouping' companies. The Great Northern Atlantics, for example, still had a distinguished future before them, and a wide variety of 4–6–0s and 4–4–0s still carried around with them the atmosphere of an earlier railway era.

At the end of its independent life, the London & South Western Railway introduced 20 4–6–0 locomotives which inspired the development of one of the most admired classes of the Southern Railway during the steam era. Designed by R W Urie, the last Motive Power Superintendent of the LSWR, the 20 4–6–0 outside-cylinder engines, with his charac-

**Above: A Great Western 'Castle' class 4–6–0 speeds the 'Cheltenham Flyer' toward London.**

**Below: An up LNER express in 1935 waits to leave Doncaster with Gresley Pacific No 4479, *Robert the Devil*.**

**Below right: The eaves of a characteristic Great Western station platform awning frame 'Castle' class 4–6–0 No 7019, *Fowey Castle*.**

**Right: After C B Collett's 'Castles' came his larger 4–6–0s, the 'Kings.' No. 6027, *King Richard 1*, hurries down the Cornish Riviera Express past Reading West station in 1938.**

teristic high running plate emphasizing their 6-foot 7-inch (2007-mm) driving wheels, all went into service between 1918 and 1923. When R E L Maunsell became Chief Mechanical Engineer of the Southern Railway in 1923 he took Urie's design as the basis of a new express passenger 4–6–0, the 'King Arthur' class, and introduced some improvements of his own. The new class was launched with ten brand-new engines built at Eastleigh. The 20 Urie engines were brought into line with them and 30 more were ordered from the North British Locomotive Company Limited. With further construction at Eastleigh, the class eventually numbered 74 engines, the last appearing in 1927. Maunsell altered the smokebox arrangements to improve the draft compared with the original Urie engines, reduced the cylinder diameter from 22 inches to 20.5 inches (559 mm to 521 mm) and raised the boiler pressure from 180 lb per square inch (12.7 kg/sq cm) to 200 lb per square inch (14.1 kg/sq cm). The valve gear was also altered to give a longer travel.

It was an astute move on the part of the Southern Railway to name express engines after the semi-legendary personage of King Arthur and his wholly legendary entourage of knights and ladies whose domain spread west from Winchester. And so the holiday trains from London's Waterloo station set out behind engines with resonant names like *Sir Mador de la Porte* or *Sir Cador of Cornwall*. Their widely scattered 'through' portions, shed at intervals as they made their way westward, sometimes came to rest at places so remote that it was hard to imagine a continuous line of rails stretching back to the banks of the Thames in London.

Far left: Britain's final prenationalization design of Pacific was Bulleid's 'West Country' class — an engine with a comparatively light axle-loading enabling it to work over the branches in the West Country and on the 'Southern's' main lines. It was, in the main, rebuilt as No 34044 *Woolacombe*.
Left: The last steam locomotive to be built for British Rail No 92220 at Shildon, 1975.
Below: British Railways' only steam-operated line, the 2-foot gauge Vale of Rheidol section out-of-Aberystwyth train.

Above: The first of Riddles' standard designs for British Railways was the 'Britannia' class medium Pacific. Produced to run over most of Britain's main lines with all but the heaviest expresses, these engines found their way from Devon to Scotland. The majority of the class carried names but the later engines were distinguishable only by their numbers, such as No 70045 standing at Skipton with a northbound fast freight.

Right: Perhaps Sir Nigel Gresley's masterpiece was this A4 class streamlined Pacific introduced in 1935 for the famous 'Silver Jubilee' express from London (King's Cross) to Edinburgh. British Rail painted the class in their standard dark green as shown here adorning No 60029, *Woodcock*.

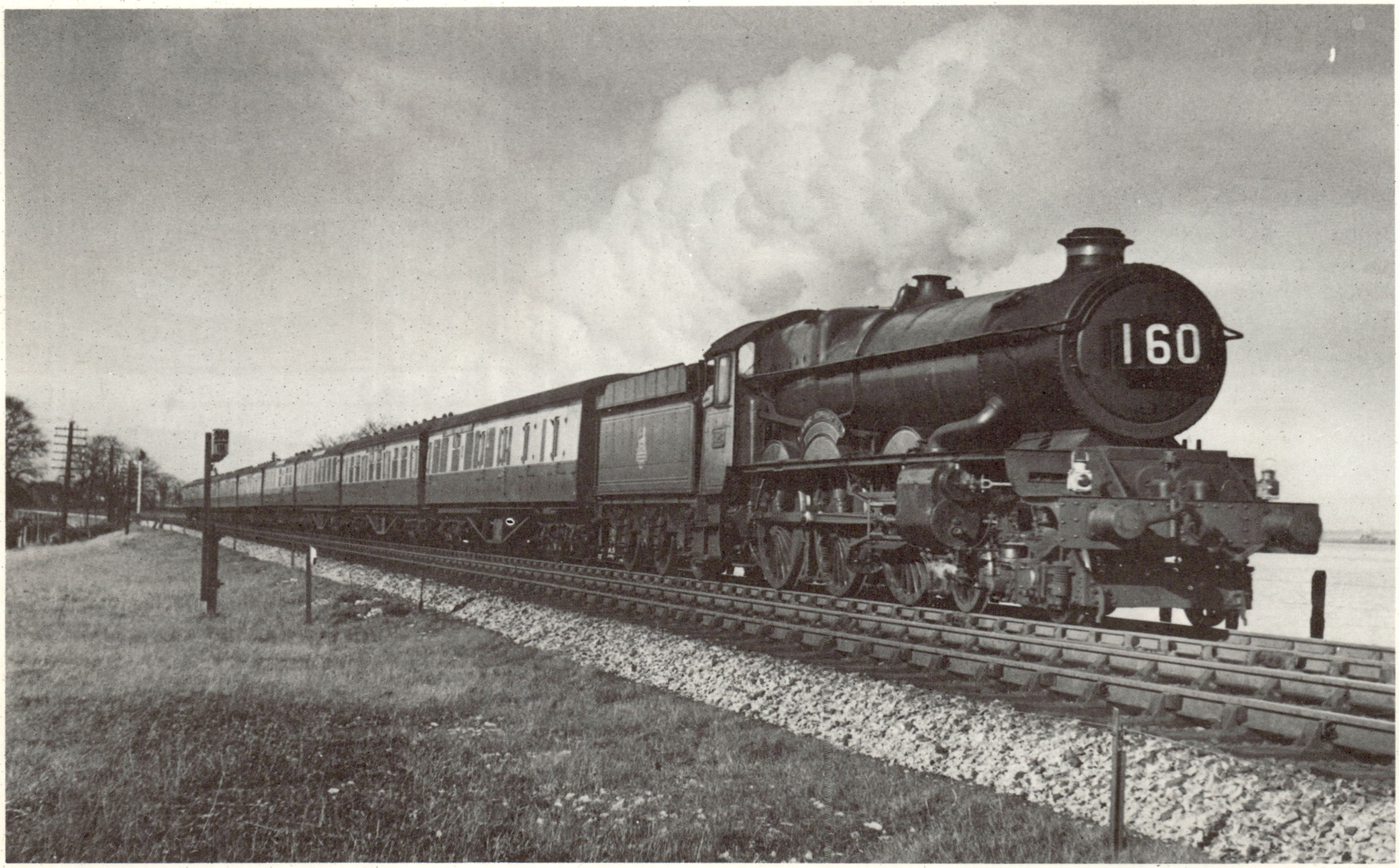
160

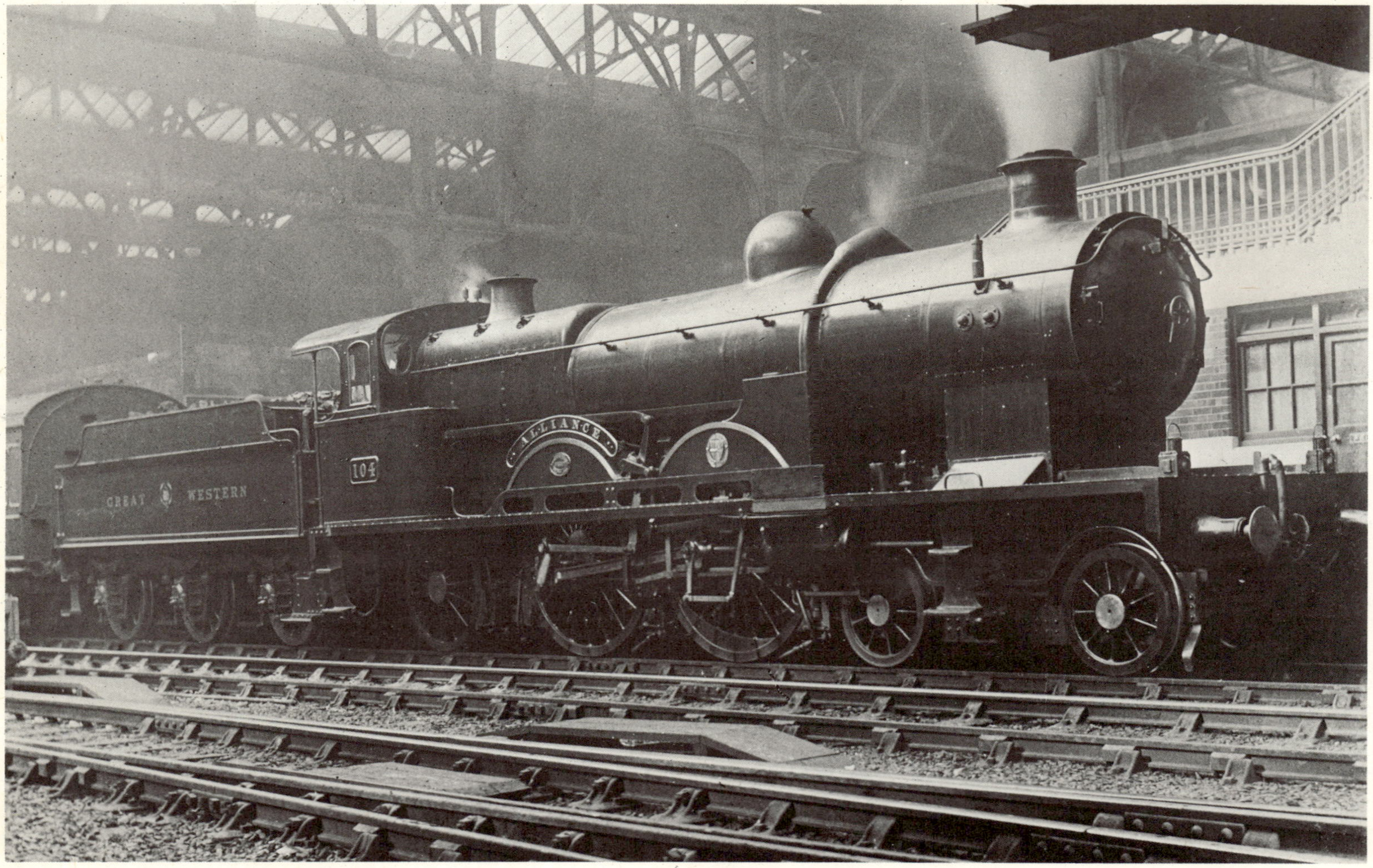
ALLIANCE
104
GREAT WESTERN

Express.' The prize of three guineas went to a guard at Waterloo whose entry was the first received, the others being rewarded with paperweight models of a 'King Arthur' class locomotive. The name lasted until 1964, when 'through' services between Waterloo and the West Country were terminated at Exeter. For most of its life the train carried coaches for Plymouth and the south Devon resorts of Seaton, Sidmouth and Exmouth as well as those for the Atlantic Coast, giving it the largest number of through portions of any train in the country. In the 1930s it was often powered by 'Lord Nelson' class locomotives between London and Salisbury, where 'King Arthurs' took over. They in turn were replaced by 4—4—0 or 2—6—0 engines of lighter axle-load for the final stages of the journey with the portions that continued past Exeter for destinations further west.

The 'King Arthurs' could not work over the main line from Tonbridge to Hastings because of restricted clearances. This was a route with heavy gradients, and the problems it presented were the primary reason for the development of a new 4—4—0 locomotive that was required to be, as far as possible, the equivalent of a contemporary 4—6—0 in all respects except adhesion. Maunsell achieved this in his 'Schools' class 4—4—0 by combining a shortened version of the 'King Arthur' boiler with the cylinders, valves and front-end design of a 'Lord Nelson' but using three cylinders instead of four. The 'Schools,' introduced in 1930, were the most powerful 4—4—0s in Europe. They equalled the 'King Arthurs' in nominal tractive effort but weighed 75 US tons/67 UK tons/68 tonnes as against the 91 US tons/81 UK tons/82 tonnes of the 4—6—0.

As well as relieving older 4—4—0s on the Hastings line, the 'Schools' enabled the Southern to increase the loading of its 80-minute Charing Cross—Folkestone trains and allowed the nonstop Waterloo—Portsmouth time to be cut to one and one-half hours for the 79.3 miles (127.6 km) in the summer timetables of 1935.

When the 'Schools' appeared in 1930 the most interesting developments in Southern steam practice were still in the future, but on one section of the railway steam was already seeing an Indian Summer. The Central Section of the Southern comprised the former London, Brighton & South Coast Railway, whose main line to Brighton was being electrified. Completion of the work at the end of 1932 made the last of the LBSCR's express locomotive designs redundant. These were the Baltic (4—6—4) tank engines designed by L Billinton, and were the ultimate expression of the old Brighton company's policy of building tank engines for its relatively short-distance express traffic as well as those for suburban services. It should be noted that it is only 51 miles (82.1 km) from London's Victoria station to Brighton but the route required smart locomotive performance to keep to the 60-minute commuter schedule as signal checks and stops in the inner-London suburban traffic area were inevitable and lost time had to be recouped in the 40 miles (64.4 km) south of East Croydon station where there were fewer junctions and speed restrictions. Billinton's Baltics were converted to 4—6—0 tender engines in 1934 and transferred to the former LSWR lines.

As electrification was extended progressively to the coastal towns of Eastbourne, Hastings and Portsmouth, other ex-Brighton passenger engines were turned over to secondary routes but the Atlantic

**Above: Southern Railway 4—6—0 No 850, *Lord Nelson*, heads for London with the 'Golden Arrow' boat train in the shadow of the famous Dover cliffs. Above left: In this 1951 view of the 'Cornish Riviera Express' near Starcross, No 6023, *King Edward II*, is painted in a blue livery. Left: In the early 1900s the Great Western Railway experimented briefly with compounding on the de Glehn system. No 104, *Alliance*, seen at Snow Hill station, was one of three 4—4—2 compounds built in France for the GWR to the order of G J Churchward for comparative trials.**

The Southern was equally fortunate in finding a romantic-sounding name for its premier service from Waterloo station to the West. In LSWR days there had been fierce competition with Great Western for Plymouth traffic, but the South Western route suffered the combined disadvantages of length and difficulty. On the other hand the company could offer a competitive service to Ilfracombe in Devon — SW had its own line to that seaside resort over which it worked through portions of Great Western trains from Paddington station in London. Further west, Bude and Padstow looked out over the Atlantic Ocean (Ilfracombe could claim to do the same if one looked in the right direction). Named trains had not proliferated in the early years after 'Grouping' though Great Western's 'Cornish Riviera Limited' was well established. A competition to find a suitable name for the mid-morning express from Waterloo to the West was launched in the *Southern Railway Magazine* and no fewer than four entrants proposed 'Atlantic Coast

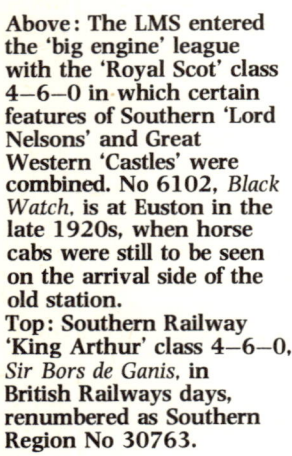

Above: The LMS entered the 'big engine' league with the 'Royal Scot' class 4—6—0 in which certain features of Southern 'Lord Nelsons' and Great Western 'Castles' were combined. No 6102, *Black Watch*, is at Euston in the late 1920s, when horse cabs were still to be seen on the arrival side of the old station.

Top: Southern Railway 'King Arthur' class 4—6—0, *Sir Bors de Ganis*, in British Railways days, renumbered as Southern Region No 30763.

locomotives designed by D E Marsh, who had been closely associated with development of the large-boilered engines of the same wheel arrangement on the Great Northern Railway, were still to be seen on the main line on the Newhaven boat train. In Southern Railway days the class was rebuilt with superheaters. They were then named after coastal headlands, including the one which had previously been *La France* in honor of the visit of the President of France in 1913. In a second series of Atlantics Marsh provided superheaters from the outset. None were named by the LBSCR but further 'headland' names were given them by the Southern.

The Southern Railway's electrification schemes only involved passenger services — freight continued to be steam hauled — and so the 2—6—0 goods engines brought out by Billinton for the LBSCR in 1913 continued in the role for which they were intended until the end of their days under British Railways.

For some reason which is hard to define, the London, Brighton & South Coast Railway enjoyed a charisma all its own. This was most deeply felt by

those who lived in or near its territories, but others could sense it. Partly perhaps it was the glamor of the all-Pullman London–Brighton express, the 'Southern Belle,' advertised as 'the most luxurious train in the world' and surviving into the electric era as the 'Brighton Belle.' However, some think the powerful Brighton appeal began with the very high standard of cleanliness insisted on for engines. Drivers were assigned their own engines and each man's name was shown on a plate fixed in the cab.

World War I was a watershed in many ways. On the railways the Chief Mechanical Engineers who took over at 'Grouping' inevitably found gaps in the capabilities of the motive power they inherited when it came to working a railway in the postwar world, and serving a public that tended to expect more and to be more critical. The move toward more powerful locomotives has been noted already. On the Great Northern section of the LNER the requirement for power gave birth to the Gresley Pacifics, but on the Great Eastern section of the same railway a 4—6—0 design was needed which would have reserve

power over existing locomotives but have the same clearance restrictions. Gresley's answer was the 'Sandringham' class, a three-cylinder locomotive using his own derived drive for the center cylinder valve gear as on his Pacifics. The first series of 'Sandringhams' were named after what are now called 'stately homes.' To meet GE section requirements they were equipped with short tenders to keep within the overall length of their predecessors. This rather spoiled their appearance, but the improvement of 19 percent over existing Great Eastern 4—6—0s was ample compensation from the point of view of the operators. Later, additional locomotives of the same class were built for the Great Central section of the LNER and fitted with much larger tenders of modern design, so that both looks and performance were of high standard.

Although Great Central was a commercial problem in that many of its services duplicated those of other main lines with shorter routes, it brought with it to the LNER some noteworthy locomotive classes. They were the legacy of J G Robinson, Chief Mechanical

Engineer of the GCR, who had given that railway a fleet of good-looking locomotives which must have done much to endow it with an up-to-the-minute image in contemporary eyes. Gresley was sufficiently impressed by the Robinson 'Director' class 4—4—0s for express traffic and his 4—6—2 tanks for fast commuter services to have more locomotives of both classes built, the 4—4—0s to supplement motive power inherited by the LNER from the North British Railway in Scotland and the tank engines to work on short distance passenger duties in the North Eastern area. In building his own 'Hunt' class 4—4—0s at a later date, Gresley chose three cylinders and his own derived valve motion for the inside cylinder but the engines embodied certain 'Director' features, particularly in the boiler proportions. A later series of 'Hunts,' beginning in 1932, was fitted with poppet valve gear.

One of Robinson's designs for Great Central was later to be seen widely on the LNER. This was his 2—8—0 freight locomotive, first put to work in 1911 on the GCR and later built in large numbers by private

**Above: C J Bowen Cooke's 'Claughton' class 4—6—0 of 1913 was the ancestor of the much more successful LMS 'Patriots' of the 1930s. 'Claughton' No 5964,** *Patriot,* **was named as a memorial to the LNWR employees who fell in World War I.**

firms for the requirements of the Railway Operating Division during World War I. Many of them were acquired by the LNER in the postwar years. In 1930, however, six-coupled classes still predominated for freight traffic, with the inside-cylinder 0–6–0 as the classic British type. The LMS had built an inside-cylinder 0–8–0 in 1929 but this was, in many respects, a development of an earlier design for the London & North Western Railway.

By 1930 the first fruits of a new motive power policy were becoming visible – namely the development of the general purpose or mixed traffic locomotive. In some quarters the 2–6–0 wheel arrangement was favored for motive power in this category. British manufacturers had long experience in building the 2–6–0 for overseas markets, where it was popular from an early period. Its beginnings in Great Britain were tentative and two of the earliest had been built for an overseas company which found itself unable to take delivery. They were bought from the builder, no doubt on favorable terms, by the impecunious Midland & South Western Junction Railway in England and when they were put into service in 1895 and 1896 they were the only representatives of this wheel arrangement in the country. Later the 2–6–0 was to be widely used, and the Great Western was building outside-cylinder 2–6–0s as early as 1911. At 'Grouping,' incidentally, it inherited the two pioneers from the MSWJR, one of which lasted until 1930.

In the early 'Grouping' years the LMS produced the versatile class of 2–6–0s popularly known as 'Crabs.' A high running plate exposed the inclined outside cylinders, valve gear and 5-foot 6-inch (1676-mm) coupled wheels. When all the rods and cranks of the Walschaerts gear were in motion the effect presumably recalled the movements of a crab's pincers to some imaginative observer.

An alternative approach to mixed traffic design was the small-wheeled version of a 4–6–0 passenger locomotive. Great Western in 1924 rebuilt a 'Saint'

Above: SR 'Schools' class 4–4–0 No 930, *Radley*, waits for the starting signal at Waterloo in the 1930s.
Above right: Ex-LBSC K class 2–6–0 No 32349 heads an Eastleigh-to-Fratton goods train on the single line from Knowle Junction to Fareham.
Left: After the Brighton main-line electrification, LBSC main-line classes found employment on secondary routes. Marsh Atlantic No 32421 leaves Selsdon with a slow train from Brighton in 1950.
Right: Soon to be displaced by electrification and rebuilt as a 4–6–0 tender engine, the former London, Brighton & South Coast Railway's war memorial engine, 4–6–4T No 333, *Remembrance*, waits with lifting safety valves to leave Victoria Station.

Left: A 'Director' class 4—4—0 of the Great Central Railway's first series. The second series and those built subsequently by the LNER had side-window cabs. No 5436, *Sir Berkeley Sheffield*, belonged to LNER class D10.
Far left: An ex-Great Central 4—6—2T, No 5447 of LNER class A5, passes Chorleywood on the Metropolitan & Great Central Joint line with a local train in June 1934.
Below: The 'Lord Faringdon' 4—6—0s of the Great Central Railway were renowned for their looks, but their performance was marred by an inadequate grate area. Under Grouping, when they became LNER class B3, they worked on other sections of the LNER. No 6164, *Earl Beatty*, on the East Coast Main Line, has a heavier load than it would normally encounter on its home metals.

class 4—6—0 with coupled wheels of 6 feet (1829 mm) diameter instead of 6 feet 8 inches (2032 mm). It was a successful experiment, and two years later the railway began production of the numerous 'Hall' class. The 'Halls' carried the same boiler as the Churchward passenger 4—6—0s and could give a good account of themselves on fast passenger work. Many mixed traffic 4—6—0s followed them in the course of the 1930s. The general-purpose locomotive was an operator's ideal which was just coming within his reach at the beginning of the decade.

It was some time before the Pacific wheel arrangement was widely adopted in Great Britain. The Great Western never returned to it after *The Great Bear*. A class of five 'Pacifics' was designed for the North Eastern Railway by Sir Vincent Raven and introduced on the eve of 'Grouping.' They came into LNER ownership in 1923 but all were withdrawn in 1936–37. Apart from these, Gresley's Pacifics were the only representatives of this wheel arrangement in a tender locomotive for a decade. The LMS soldiered on for a time with its 'Royal Scot' 4—6—0s as its first line express locomotives, but when Sir Henry Fowler was succeeded by W A (later Sir William) Stanier it received its first Pacific design.

Observers at the first appearance of the Stanier Pacific saw not only a pair of wheels under the firebox but also a tapered boiler, the hallmark of a Great Western locomotive. The first two Stanier Pacifics were not outstandingly successful. They had a moderate degree of superheat, the idea being to improve thermal efficiency by minimizing waste heat in the exhaust. In Great Western conditions, the firm from which Stanier had come, this practice had worked well, but on the much less homogeneous LMS, where the quality of coal often differed from area to area and there was a diversity of driving practice, Stanier's designs tended at first to be unsatisfactory steamers. Later engines of the class were given higher superheat and in due course the two originals were modified accordingly. This improved version was the basis of the ultimate in express locomotive development by Sir William Stanier.

In the 1920s the emphasis had been on locomotive power but at the turn of the decade railway publicity changed to concentrate on the more marketable commodity of speed. There had been numerous speed highlights already, but the overall pattern was patchy and in 1931 the mileage scheduled to be covered daily at speeds between 60 and 70 mph (97 and 113 kph) was only 861 miles (1385.6 km). A year later it rose to 2134 miles (3434.3 km).

For some years after World War I the fastest scheduled run in the British Isles was made by a train on the North Eastern Railway which was required to cover the 44.1 miles (70.9 km) from Darlington to York in 43 minutes (61.7 mph/99.3 kph). In 1923 when the North Eastern had become part of the LNER Group, the Great Western took the record from it by booking the 14.30 from Cheltenham to run the 77.1 miles (124.1 km) from Swindon to Paddington in 75 minutes (61.8 mph/99.4 kph). This was before the advent of the 'Castles' but Great Western 4—6—0s of earlier classes often improved on the scheduled time.

When new engines were available, Great Western in 1929 was able to schedule the train to run from Swindon to Paddington in 70 minutes, pushing the average speed up to 66.3 mph (106.7 kph), and enabling Great Western to claim ownership of 'the

Above: A local train on the Somerset & Dorset Joint line in British Railways days is headed by an example of the classic British inside-cylinder 0-6-0 for freight work. No 44102 in this picture was an LMS development of a Midland Railway design.
Above right: 'Hunt' class 4-4-0 No 235, *The Bedale*, was one of a series of engines designed by Gresley in which he used three cylinders and his own valve gear but incorporated certain features of the GC 'Director' class.
Right: A Great Western '43' 2-6-0 No 4367 looks as much at home under express headcode as on any of the duties this versatile early mixed-traffic class was called upon to undertake.

fastest train in the world.' The title suddenly slipped away, however, for in Canada at this time the fierce competition for traffic between Montreal and Toronto led the Canadian Pacific Railway to accelerate two trains to run the 124 miles (200 km) between Smith's Falls and Toronto at average speeds of 68.9 and 67.6 mph (110.9 and 108.8 kph). In response the Great Western reacted by cutting three minutes off the Swindon–Paddington schedule, achieving an average speed of 69.2 mph (111.4 kph). Once more it had 'the fastest train in the world' and in case the fact was overlooked by the public, a headboard suitably inscribed was carried by the locomotive. The train had become generally known as the 'Cheltenham Flyer' although the name did not appear in the timetable. The final acceleration came in 1932 when the time for the 77.1 miles (124.1 km) was cut to 65 minutes and the average speed rose to 77.1 mph (124.1 kph). All these scheduled times and speeds were improved upon on various occasions, culminating in the so-called 'record of records' of 5 June 1932 when Number 5006, *Tregenna Castle*, took the train from Swindon to Paddington in 56 minutes 47 seconds, giving an average of 81.7 mph (131.4 kph).

The 'Cheltenham Flyer' was not balanced by a corresponding service in the opposite direction, and in any case it only 'flew' from Swindon to London on generally falling gradients. Its schedule from Chelten-

ham to Swindon was quite mundane.

Although the Anglo-Scottish services were the most prestigious of the British express trains, their speed was restrained for many years by an agreement between the West Coast and East Coast companies following an accident at Preston in 1895 when a West Coast express had been derailed by taking the curve through the station at excessive speed.

For 37 years the companies concerned limited their London–Glasgow and London–Edinburgh trains to a minimum time of 8.25 hours. The advent of larger locomotives in the 1920s inevitably brought a new stirring of the competitive spirit, but at first it had to be expressed in a different way. In 1927 an advance portion of the 'Flying Scotsman' King's Cross (London)-Edinburgh express of the LNER began running nonstop between London and Newcastle (268.5 miles/432.1 km) behind Gresley's Pacifics. The rival LMS responded by deleting from the public timetable all intermediate stops by its 10.00 express in each direction between Euston and Glasgow. These trains were also shown in the timetable for the first time as the 'Royal Scot,' which eventually ran nonstop from Euston to Kingmoor (Carlisle), a distance of 301 miles (484.4 km).

Early in 1928 the LNER announced that beginning with the summer timetable the 'Flying Scotsman' would run nonstop in both directions between King's

Cross and Edinburgh. This was to be a genuine nonstop run of 393 miles (632.5 km). For its daily performance provision had to be made for changing engine crews *en route*, and for this purpose certain Pacifics were equipped with tenders having a corridor along one side and the usual form of intercoach vestibule connection at the rear, so that a relief crew riding in the leading compartment of the train could walk through to the footplate and take over at the halfway point of the journey.

Nonstop runs to Scotland by its rival put the LMS in a difficult position because the 'Royal Scot' had to stop *en route* to Glasgow to detach the Edinburgh portion. But the company was determined not to be outdone: a few days before the nonstop 'Flying Scotsman' was introduced, the 'Royal Scot' was run from Euston in two portions, one for Edinburgh and one for Glasgow, and both were worked to their destinations without a stop. Each locomotive carried a crew of three, one man as a reserve. The eight-coach Glasgow portion was worked by 'Royal Scot' class 4—6—0 No 6113, *Cameronian*, but the lighter six-coach portion for Edinburgh was headed by compound 4—4—0 No 1054. The 393.7 miles (633.6 km) nonstop from Euston to Edinburgh's Princes Street on this occasion exceeded any previous nonstop run by a British four-coupled locomotive by 100 miles (161 km).

Left: A long-lived Great
Western 'Saint' class
4—6—0 No 2915 heads an
express near Knowle &
Dorridge on 14 May 1949.
A rebuild of a 'Saint' in
1924 paved the way to
the 'Hall' and other GW
4—6—0 general-purpose
classes.

Such a lengthy stint for the enginemen could not become a permanent feature and the LMS reverted to engine-changing outside Carlisle until the coming of the first Stanier Pacifics on the LMS in 1933.

When the anomalous 8.25-hour agreement between companies was dropped from the summer of 1932, the 'Royal Scot' ran to Glasgow in 7 hours 40 minutes and the 'Flying Scotsman' to Edinburgh in 7 hours 30 minutes. Both timings had been improved by 1939 when the outbreak of war put an end to competitive acceleration, but by that time the fastest Anglo-Scottish journeys were being made by new streamlined trains.

By 1938 the mileage run at over 60 mph (97 kph) in Great Britain had risen to 11,665 miles (18,773 km); and at over 70 mph (113 kph) to 730 miles (1174.8 km), all with steam traction.

Gresley of the LNER had been attracted by the idea of a high-speed business service and had an open mind over the choice of steam or diesel-electric as motive power. In 1934 he made a report to the LNER Board which led to a party of the company's officers, including himself, visiting Germany to explore the possibility of high-speed diesel-electric services on the East Coast main line, initially between London, Leeds and Newcastle, modelled on those of the Deutsche Reichsbahn. However, Gresley then decided against a gamble with untried engines and decided to see what could be done with steam traction and a locomotive-and-coaches train.

The first experiment was made on 30 November 1934 with the Pacific locomotive No 4472, *Flying Scotsman* and a four-coach train on a journey from London to Leeds and back. Going north the train covered the 185.7 miles (298.8 km) in 152 minutes and ran for over 70 miles (112.6 km) at an average speed in excess of 80 mph (129 kph). The maximum attained was 95 mph (153 kph). The homeward trip was distinguished by a brief 100 mph (161 kph) burst of speed recorded in the dynamometer car while descending a 1-in-200 gradient. Probably the maximum was not held for more than 600 yards (550 m) but it caused great excitement because of the rarity of authenticated three-figure speeds in British railway history. (A maximum of 102.3 mph [164.6 kph] attained early in the century on the Great Western Railway, and long accepted, was closely scrutinized in later years and some doubt was cast on its accuracy.)

On 5 March 1935 a further high-speed trial was conducted, this time between London and Newcastle, 268.3 miles (431.8 km) each way. The locomotive, heading a six-coach train, was Pacific No 2750, *Papyrus,* one of the later Gresley Pacifics with a 220 lb per square inch (15.5 kg/sq cm) boiler. The schedule in both directions was 240 minutes, which was cut to 237 minutes going north and 232 minutes returning, but the climax of the day occurred as the train hurried south through Lincolnshire, once more aided by the descent at 1-in-200 from Stoke tunnel. A commentator wrote, 'At last the magic "hundred" has been passed, and this time in a way that admits of no dispute. Not only was the enormously high figure of 108 mph (174 kph) maintained for ten seconds continuously, but for 12.3 miles (19.8 km), from Corby down to Tallington, the speed *averaged* 100.6 mph (161.9 kph).'

At the LNER annual general meeting in 1935 the company's chairman cautiously announced that 'serious consideration' would be given to the 'possible' introduction of four-hour services between London's King's Cross and Newcastle in the next timetable. Matters were, in fact, advancing rapidly. The suggestion of a high-speed steam train for the London–Newcastle service was made by Sir Ralph Wedgwood, Chief General Manager of the LNER, after the trial

Below: A southbound train via Oxford and Reading waits at Birmingham Snow Hill behind GW 'Hall' class 4–6–0 No 5959, *Mawley Hall*, in 1955.

runs of 5 March. Gresley submitted an outline diagram of a suggested train on 11 March, which was shown to the Board and approved on 28 March. The necessary orders for the design and construction of locomotives and coaches were given to the works at Doncaster forthwith. No doubt the haste was due in part to the fact that 1935 was the Silver Jubilee of the reign of King George V and therefore a fitting occasion for demonstrating British engineering skill and inventiveness.

The new train of seven coaches and streamlined Pacific locomotive was ready for a demonstration run on 27 September 1935. It entered public service with the name 'Silver Jubilee' three days later. The demonstration run showed that 100 mph (161 kph) speeds could soon become commonplace on special streamlined trains of restricted weight. The 100 mph (161 kph) mark was passed going north only 30 miles (48.3 km) out of London and speed did not fall below that level for the next 25 miles (40.2 km). A maximum of 112.5 mph (181 kph) was reached at two separate points.

The four new Pacific locomotives built initially for the streamlined trains had similar valve gear, driving wheel diameter and wheelbase spacing to the standard engines but some boiler proportions were

Far left below: The smokebox nameplate of streamlined Pacific No 4496, *Golden Shuttle*, is clearly visible in this view of the down 'Coronation' King's Cross—Edinburgh express about to be engulfed in a tunnel. *Golden Shuttle* was allocated to the West Riding Limited streamliner (King's Cross—Leeds—Bradford) in September 1937.

Below: LNER streamlined Pacific No 2510, *Quicksilver*, heads the 'Silver Jubilee' King's Cross—Newcastle express. Far left above: This early view of No 2510 at rest recalls the period when the names of the first streamliners were painted at the center of the boiler casing instead of appearing on a smokebox nameplate.

changed. In the design of steam and exhaust passages Gresley followed principles which had been successfully applied by André Chapelon in rebuilding Pacific locomotives in France. It was not, in fact, Gresley's first venture in this direction, for he had acted similarly in building his large 2–8–2 express locomotives for Scotland's Edinburgh–Aberdeen route. There was much argument as to whether this 'internal streamlining' was not more important than the external streamlining. Comparative wind-tunnel tests on wooden models of streamlined and nonstreamlined locomotives were carried out at the National Physical Laboratory and the results suggested that streamlining could be worth a saving of 100 hp in the average output required between London's King's Cross station and Newcastle but it proved difficult to substantiate this figure in practice.

In 1937 streamlining spread to the Anglo-Scottish services, already lively compared with their long slumber under the 8.25-hour agreement. Now the LMS entered the field, building five new Pacific locomotives basically similar to those introduced by Stanier in 1933 but with certain modifications and a beautiful streamlined exterior. Their immediate purpose was to work the 'Coronation Scot' streamlined express between London and Glasgow, but more were built later, both with and without streamlining, for general heavy express passenger duties. King George V had died in 1936. The following year saw the coronation of King George VI, hence the name of the new LMS Anglo-Scottish streamliner

and one of the LNER's 'Coronation' streamlined London–Edinburgh expresses which entered service at the same time, again hauled by Gresley's streamlined Pacifics. More of these engines were being built at the time and those allocated to the 'Coronation' service were painted Garter blue. The 'Coronation Scot' ran between London's Euston Station and Glasgow in six and one-half hours and the 'Coronation' between King's Cross Station and Edinburgh in only six hours.

Stanier's Pacifics for the 'Coronation Scot' were more than a streamlined version of his earlier 'Princess Royal' class 4–6–2s. Instead of four sets of Walschaerts valve gears, the gears for the outside cylinders operated the valves of the inside cylinders through rocking levers, and the piston valves were of 9-inch (229 mm) diameter instead of 8 inches (203 mm). Coupled wheel diameter was increased from 6 feet 6 inches to 6 feet 9 inches (1981 mm to 2057 mm). As Gresley had done in his streamliners, Stanier paid special attention to the free flow of steam. The locomotives for the 'Coronation Scot' service had a streamlined external casing and were known as the 'Princess Coronation' class, a name which linked them with their 'Princess Royal' predecessors. Further locomotives of the same design were built without streamlining. These were the 'Duchess' class. In the 'Princess Coronations' and the 'Duchesses' the heating surface was increased from the previous 2967 square feet (275.6 sq m) in the 'Princess Royals' to 3637 square feet (337.9 sq m). By using

Above: One of the early Stanier Pacifics, No 6204, *Princess Louise*, takes a northbound LMS express past Linslade, Buckinghamshire, in 1936. A rather dirty 'semaphore'-type Scottish route indicator is just visible on the smokebox.

**Above: One of the streamlined versions of the Stanier Pacifics No 6223, *Princess Alice*, heads the LMS 'Coronation Scot' London–Glasgow service in 1938.**

nickel steel the thickness of the boiler and firebox plates was significantly reduced, and in spite of the larger heating surface a nonstreamlined 'Duchess' weighed slightly under a ton more than a 'Princess Royal' weighed.

The 'Coronation Scot' made a demonstration run from Euston (London) to Crewe and back on 29 June 1937. The occasion is remembered for the dramatic acceleration over the last eight miles (12.8 km) into Crewe. As far as Whitmore the train had not exceeded 87.5 mph (140.8 kph) at any point but the authorities were evidently determined to make the most of the favorable conditions between Whitmore and Crewe in order to surpass the 112.5 mph (181 kph) achieved by LNER's 'Silver Jubilee' on its demonstration run two years earlier. The goal was reached, but only at the last moment, a peak of 114 mph (184 kph) being attained with the train already uncomfortably close to Crewe. With only a half-mile (0.8 km) left before reaching the crossovers at the approach to the station the train braked very sharply and lurched over the crossovers in dramatic style.

But Gresley was not content to leave speed honors with the LMS. The role of the brakes in high-speed running is often overlooked, but stopping distances are of the utmost importance and it is equally important to minimize the delay in application of brakes between front and rear vehicles, inherent in the vacuum system. In 1938 the LNER was conducting trials with a new type of brake valve. The locomotive

in use for this purpose on 3 July was streamlined Pacific No 4468 *Mallard* with a train of six 'Coronation' coaches. While descending the 1-in-200 of Stoke bank the engine was opened up to the limit and for a moment the speed recorder in the dynamometer car showed 126 mph (203 kph). However, during the run a big end on *Mallard* overheated and the engine was taken off the train at Peterborough.

The plaque commemorating the 'famous victory' was not affixed to *Mallard* until 1948. It can still be seen on the locomotive, now preserved in the National Railway Museum at York, and reads, 'On the 3rd July 1938 this locomotive attained a world speed record for steam traction of 126 miles per hour.'

The golden age of the streamlined train ended with the outbreak of World War II but the locomotives built to work them gave good service for many years, with their streamlining either modified to allow easier access to working parts or removed entirely.

Although the LMS waited until the Coronation year, 1937, to introduce a streamliner, it had marked the Silver Jubilee year, 1935, by naming one of its new 4–6–0 express passenger locomotives, *Silver Jubilee*. This was No 5552 of the class introduced by Stanier in 1934 and soon known universally as the 'Jubilees.' It appeared in a black and silver livery instead of the normal LMS red with yellow lining. The Jubilees were part of the huge program of updating LMS motive power which Stanier shouldered on his appointment to the railway.

After Fowler's 'Royal Scots,' further 4–6–0s had

been provided by rebuilding certain engines of the former LNWR 'Claughton' class and by new construction programs. They became known as the 'Baby Scots,' a name deplored by the LMS but which proved hard to stamp out in favor of the officially preferred 'Patriot' class. The 'Patriots' were successful engines, but they had their roots in the past, and Stanier's job was to produce a new range of modern, standard types. His 'Jubilees' were intended as an improvement on the 'Patriots' and in the long term they proved an admirable express engine for duties below the Pacific level, although they had steaming problems in their early days and underwent a number of boiler modifications.

In the 1930s the economic problems of running a railway were beginning to bite. The ideal of a general-purpose locomotive able to turn its hand to most types of work and so be productive *throughout* its hours in steam, was becoming increasingly attractive in railway board rooms. The Great Western had moved in this direction as early as 1911 with its 4300 class 2–6–0, an efficient performer on slow or express freights or on passenger trains at speeds up to 70 mph (113 kph). In the 1930s numbers of mixed-traffic 4–6–0s were built for the GWR, equally adaptable and better equipped for the higher-speed end of their duties by reason of the leading bogie. In

this climate a mixed-traffic design was an obvious necessity for the new locomotive program on the LMS, and in 1934 Stanier produced the first of his mixed-traffic 4–6–0s of a class which ranged widely over the whole LMS system, and indeed was to become ubiquitous on British Railways until the end of steam. It was known to its admirers as the 'Black Fives.' The official classification of these engines was 5P5F, that is power class 5 for passenger and freight duties. Coupled wheel diameter was 6 feet (1829 mm) as against the 6 feet 9 inches (2057 mm) of the 'Jubilees' but they were timed on many occasions at speeds of 90 mph (145 kph) and over.

The free flow of steam obtained by 'internal streamlining' of the steam passages made high piston speeds possible. Designers could therefore use wheels of smaller diameter in locomotives which would spend some of their time on express work, and at the same time the smaller wheels gave increased tractive effort. These factors helped to create the much-desired 'general purpose' locomotive. In later years the description 'general purpose' was preferred to 'mixed-traffic' because the latter had come, by association, to imply suitability for two classes of freight work – the slow goods not fitted with continuous brakes and the fitted express freight train – rather than the whole range of duties.

Above: With streamlining removed after the war, Stanier Pacific No 46220, *Coronation*, passes Bulkington with the up 'Royal Scot' in 1949.
Above right: Stanier 'Jubilee' class 4–6–0 No 5649 stands at Derby shortly after delivery and still without its 'Hawkins' nameplates.
Right: The name of LMS No 5902, *Sir Frank Ree*, is the only recognizable sign of its being reconstructed from the similarly-named LNWR 'Claughton.' The early rebuilds and later new locomotives formed the LMS 'Patriot' class. Views such as this, before smoke deflectors were fitted, are rare.

Gresley's general-purpose locomotive for the LNER evoked considerable interest when it appeared in 1936 because it had the unusual wheel arrangement, for a tender engine, of 2–6–2, which had previously been used in Great Britain only for tank engines. The first of the class was named *Green Arrow*, identifying the design closely with the 'Green Arrow' express freight service. However, the locomotives also took their share of fast passenger trains. Gresley had already introduced his 'Cock o' the North' class of 2–8–2 passenger engines for the heavy trains on the steeply graded Edinburgh–Aberdeen route, using 6 feet 2 inches (1880 mm) coupled wheels, and he used the same wheel diameter on the 'Green Arrows' (otherwise known as the Y2 class). The 'Green Arrow' boiler was a shortened version of the one used in his second series of Pacifics and the same wide firebox made a trailing axle necessary. At the front end he placed a two-wheel truck of the same design as in an earlier and numerous class of 2–6–0s. The cab front was wedged shaped, as in the streamlined Pacifics, where the shape had been adopted for aerodynamic reasons.

A few years after their introduction the 'Green

Arrows' were called upon to perform prodigious feats of haulage in wartime traffic. One noteworthy occasion was reported in a contemporary magazine in 1940:

'Whilst it has recently been necessary to place a limit on the size of trains, there have been occasions during the past few months when LNER locomotives have accomplished stupendous feats of strength.

Greatest of all was when Green Arrow type mixed traffic locomotive No 4800 recently *hauled a passenger train of 26 vehicles weighing 762 tons from Peterborough to London.* With passengers and luggage the load hauled *exceeded a total of 800 tons and easily eclipsed all previous records.*'

The Southern Railway at this period had some small-wheeled versions of express passenger engines in service for fast freight traffic but they did not show the versatility of the specialized general-purpose design. However, a locomotive of this category was in the offing when war was declared in 1939 for Maunsell's successor, O V S Bulleid, was building a Pacific to improve on the haulage power and speed of the 'Lord Nelsons.' He chose 6-foot 2-inch (1880-mm) coupled wheels, which had by then shown themselves adequate for speeds in the 90 mph (145 kph) range, and it was fortunate that he did so for it enabled the engines to be classed as 'general purpose' so that construction was allowed to continue in the war years, when the building of locomotives purely for express passenger traffic was halted.

The first Bulleid Pacific came out in 1942. Its exterior was 'streamlined' in the eyes of the multitude, but the Southern preferred to call it 'air-smoothed.' There was a certain angularity about it, and in later years the various versions of the design came to be known as 'Spam cans,' recalling a canned meat consumed, *faute de mieux*, in large quantities during World War II. More formally, the first engines were the 'Merchant Navies,' being named after the famous shipping lines.

There were several unusual features in this class which at once earned its designer a reputation for originality. The most debatable was the special design of valve gear adopted to allow the sets for the three cylinders all to be accommodated between the frames. The gear was operated from a crankshaft which was chain driven from the main crank axle and the whole

mechanism was enclosed in an oil bath. Problems ensued and the arrangement was not popular with maintenance staff. Two series of lighter 'air-smoothed' Pacifics — the 'West Country' and 'Battle of Britain' classes — followed at the end of the war, but their maintenance record was poor and in the end all the originals and many of their smaller successors were rebuilt with conventional valve gear, and the air-smoothing construction removed.

Other departures from standard British practice in the years between the two World Wars may be noted. Gresley decided to experiment with a water tube boiler and built a 4–6–4 locomotive to take it, the boiler itself being built by an outside engineering firm. Pressure was 450 lb per square inch (31.6 kg/sq cm). In 1930 the locomotive worked passenger turns from Gateshead (Newcastle) and on one occasion made a return trip from Edinburgh to London with the non-stop 'Flying Scotsman.' Practical problems soon arose in maintaining a marine-type boiler in railway service and the experiment was short-lived, but the locomotive was rebuilt with a conventional Pacific boiler and streamlining and continued in service until 1938. A still higher working pressure — 900 lb per square inch (63.3 kg/sq cm) — was chosen for an experiment with a 'Royal Scot' type locomotive of the LMS. The locomotive was a compound; the center cylinder took high-pressure steam and exhausted it into a mixing chamber where it met with steam generated at 250 lb per square inch (17.6 kg/sq cm) in the part of the boiler built on conventional lines. During trials a pipe in the high-pressure section failed, causing an explosion in which a member of the test staff was killed. The experiment was then halted and never resumed.

A more successful venture was Stanier's turbine-driven Pacific locomotive for the LMS, built in 1935. The 'Turbomotive' as it was called showed itself able to perform as well as the best of the standard Pacifics but unfortunately much of its working life occurred under war conditions when its availability did not match that of the conventional machines and, since the turbines were made by an outside firm which was heavily engaged in war work, there were problems in obtaining spare parts. Many engineers would have liked to see the locomotive working under normal conditions after initial difficulties had been solved, but in 1946 it was rebuilt as a standard LMS Pacific. Six years later it was wrecked in a three-train collision at Harrow and had to be scrapped.

Above left: Bulleid's 'Merchant Navy' Pacifics for the Southern Railway were deemed general-purpose locomotives when they came out in the war years, but from 1946 were soon at the head of the company's crack passenger trains. In British Rail days No 35009, *Shaw Savill,* starts the up 'Atlantic Coast Express' after the Salisbury stop.
Above: Stanier turbine-driven Pacific No 6202 (the 'turbomotive') is at Rugby with a down Liverpool express in 1945. Right: LNER general-purpose 2–6–2 No 4771, *Green Arrow,* first of a class which performed notably both on express freight and fast passenger work.

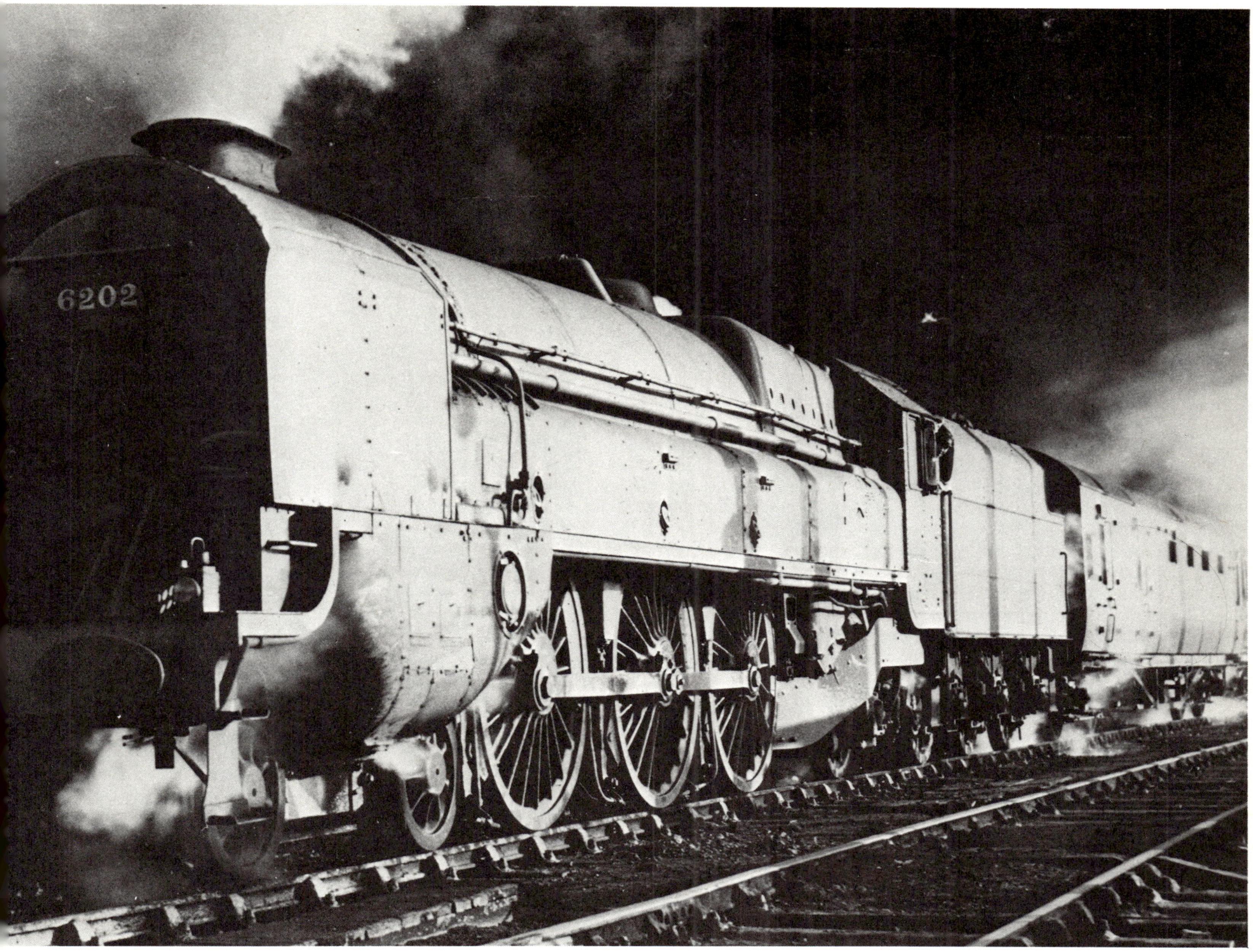
6202

GREEN ARROW
4771
L N E R

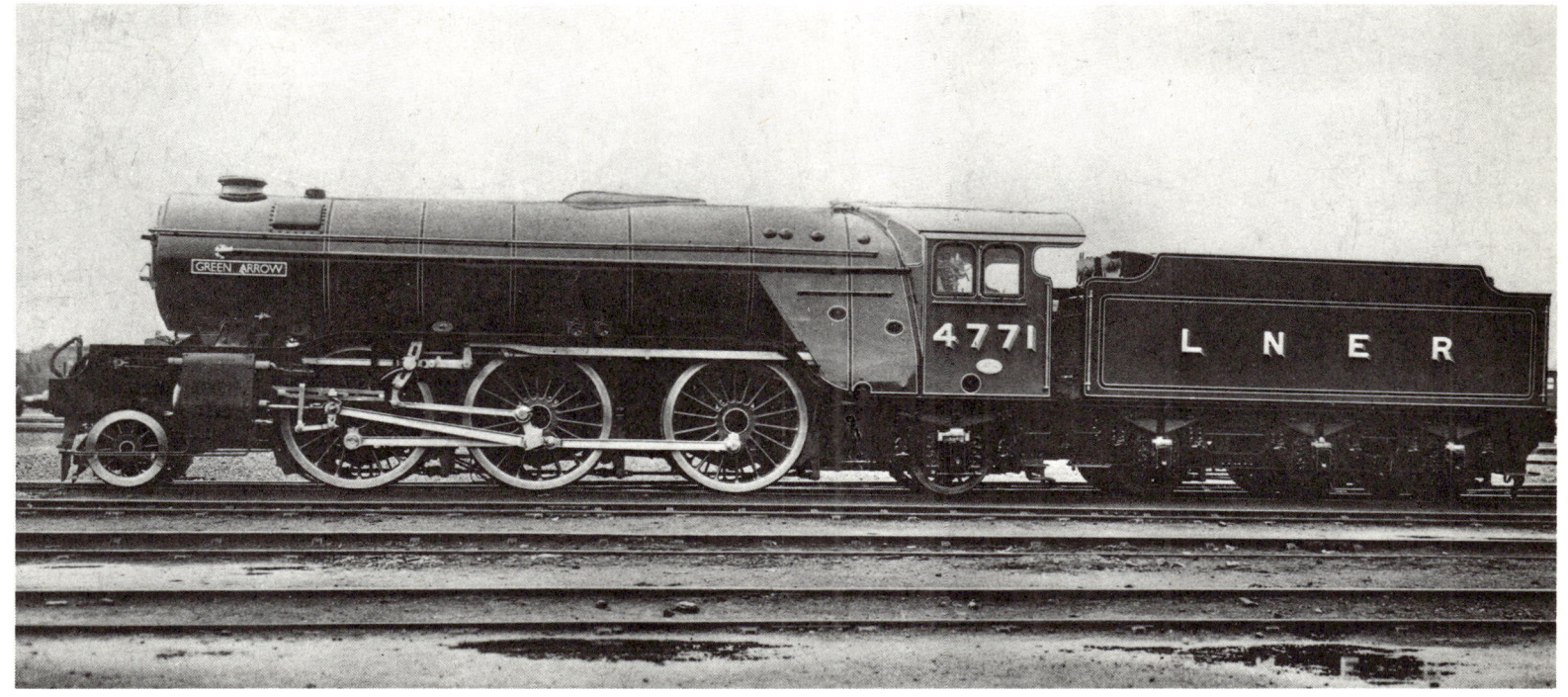

# 2. Last Steam in Britain

On 1 January 1948 the principal railways in Great Britain were nationalized. There was some joyful tooting of engine whistles at midnight on New Year's Eve, for such an event had long been desired in some quarters and there were many on the railways who had come to look upon it as a solution to all problems. Some problems, however, could not be solved overnight such as the fact that British railway motive power had been overworked for six years and had suffered from restricted maintenance.

Steam clearly had a continuing role but opinions differed as to how long. The steam locomotive was approaching the limits of what could be extracted from a mobile steam-generating plant subject to limitations on its size. It had been shown that the steam locomotive was capable of improvement beyond what had once been thought possible, but its performance in these higher regions was dependent on expert handling. In postwar conditions a locomotive would inevitably be driven by a number of crews of varying capability; simplicity rather than refinement would have to be the keynote of future design.

British Railways, as the nationalized undertaking was called, took over some 20,000 locomotives of 448 different types from the previous four railway companies. Many of these dated back to the 120 individual companies which had been amalgamated to form four 'Groups' in 1923. Such variety was unacceptable for the new unified system, where uniform maintenance procedures were to be followed and reductions in the variety of spare parts were imperative.

The first move was to decide which of the more recent locomotive classes had the best claim to become the basis for future building. This was to be settled by interchange trials in which locomotives would operate on routes outside their normal territories, and all aspects of performance would be carefully monitored. The comparisons were not made using data gleaned from special test runs, but from performance statistics taken from trains on the normal timetable. The trials took place in 1948, but revealed that no one class was outstandingly superior over all the others. Accordingly it was decided to develop a range of new standard designs to work alongside the more recent existing classes and to compensate for the withdrawals of obsolescent types.

There was some criticism of the decision to build new steam locomotives in such numbers at so late a date, but the railways had to be kept going and there was little experience of diesel or electric traction to

Left: Thompson B1 class
general-purpose 4—6—0
No 1159 stands at
Leicester Central station in
1947.

Above: British Railways
Class A1 Pacific No 60126,
*Sir Vincent Raven,* heads
the up 'Queen of Scots'
(Glasgow–Edinburgh–
King's Cross) Pullman.
The A1s were new
locomotives built by
A H Peppercorn as a
development of E
Thompson's conversion of
the original Gresley
Pacific *Great Northern.*

build on. Diesel development had concentrated on shunting units. Main-line electrification had been confined to passenger services on short-distance routes between London and the south coast, using multiple-unit trains exclusively until early in the war – after the war the grand total of three electric locomotives appeared. Moreover, Great Britain was rich in coal and, although some of the best quality grades for raising steam were running out or were reserved for export, what remained was still the envy of many Continental and overseas railwaymen.

By the time the first of the new standard locomotives was ready, modifications to certain classes

of prewar locomotives had already taken place giving them a new lease of life. Sir Nigel Gresley, Chief Mechanical Engineer of the London & North Eastern Railway, had died in 1941. He was succeeded by Edward Thompson, who had to tackle a problem which had developed in Gresley's type of valve gear for three-cylinder locomotives. With the inevitable lowering of standards and infrequency of maintenance during the war years, play had developed in the joints of the lever system which worked the valves of the inside cylinder so that the distribution of steam to all three cylinders was unbalanced. In Gresley's layout the connecting rods of the outside and inside cylinders were of unequal length — the inclined inside cylinder was shorter than the outside ones. Thompson adopted the principle that all coupling rods should be of equal length and rebuilt one of Gresley's 2—8—2s as a Pacific with an altered cylinder layout to give this effect, with separate valve gear for the inside cylinder. The difficulty experienced with Gresley's gear was removed and the other 2—8—2s were rebuilt, followed by some new Pacifics built along similar lines in 1946.

A year later A H Peppercorn succeeded Thompson as Chief Mechanical Engineer. He introduced a new Pacific in which he returned to a more orthodox cylinder layout but retained the separate gear for the inside cylinder valves.

Admirers of Sir Nigel Gresley outside the railway industry were aghast at Thompson's treatment of his locomotives and indignation reached a crescendo when he laid his hands on the historic *Great Northern*, first of the Gresley Pacifics, to modify it according to his own ideas. It seems that eyebrows were discreetly raised within the industry as well, for Sir Ronald Matthews, Chairman of the London and North Eastern Railway, was once heard to say that 'the LNER could not build a locomotive policy on the basis that everything that Gresley did was wrong.' It must be said in Thompson's defense that he acted as he did in pursuance of a policy of standardization to make the best use of available funds, which on the LNER were less than those available to Stanier on the LMS. Thompson therefore proposed to introduce certain new classes for future building, to select others which would be retained in service by reboilering, and to designate others which would only be kept in traffic until the stocks of boilers on hand were used up.

His own original contribution was the class B1 general-purpose 4—6—0 of 1942, which filled a gap in the motive power left by Gresley in that it was more closely equivalent than any of Gresley's designs to the LMS 'Black Five.' The B1 was a straightforward two-cylinder locomotive which implemented Thompson's standardization ideas by embodying many parts corresponding to existing classes so that little new machinery was needed to produce it. Over 200 B1s were built and they did excellent and varied work both during and after the war.

With the return of more normal conditions in 1945, both in maintenance and train loading, the Gresley valve gear was no longer a problem and the earlier Pacifics returned to the lighter and faster passenger services. The Thompson and Peppercorn classes had met the needs of their day but in the more tranquil postwar environment they proved less economical in fuel consumption than the older engines because of the large grate areas with which they had been endowed to meet the demands of heavy wartime traffic. Nonstop running between London's King's Cross and Edinburgh, resumed in 1948, was always entrusted to the Gresley streamlined A4 Pacifics and these engines worked the 'Elizabethan' 6.5-hour London—Edinburgh express which was the postwar equivalent of the 'Coronation' although no longer formed of special streamlined stock.

On the LMS a 'Royal Scot' locomotive had been rebuilt with an improved steam circuit and tapered boiler in 1935. The experiment was successful, and in 1943 the rebuilding of the class on similar lines but with further improvements based on the Stanier Pacifics was undertaken. In their rebuilt form the 'Royal Scots' put up some of the best performances

Left: Rebuilt 'Royal Scot' class 4—6—0 No 6108, *Seaforth Highlander,* leaves Carlisle. The locomotive is in the glossy black livery once used by the London & North Western Railway and revived for a time by the LMSR.

Above: In early BR days several Stanier 'Black Fives' were experimentally modified in various ways to improve their efficiency. No 44755 has been equipped with Caprotti valve gear, Timken roller bearings and double chimney.

of their career. Similar success attended the rebuilding of the 'Patriot' class from 1946 with tapered boilers, larger cylinders and a double blastpipe.

The postwar rebuilding of Southern's 'Merchant Navy' and subsequent Pacifics designed by O V S Bulleid was mentioned in Chapter One. During the war Bulleid again showed his originality and disregard for convention when he designed an 0–6–0 goods engine which had the widest possible route availability on the Southern Railway. Instead of building more of Maunsell's Q class engines, he decided that a larger boiler and firebox would be desirable. In so doing he used up a higher proportion of the overall weight than usual and so had to cut down in other directions. He eliminated the running plates and developed a cab fabricated from thin sheet. The result was very much a 'basic' locomotive, the Q1 class, with its wheels fully exposed. To go with the multiple-jet blastpipe there was a stubby chimney and the dome was similarly austere. Both of these boiler fittings were the antithesis of the shapely appurtenances on which many locomotive designers prided themselves and which were characteristic of the British locomotive for many years. Bulleid did

not do these things to shock. He had the practical end of weight saving in view. It seems likely that criticisms of the appearance of the Q1 locomotive did not cause him much concern; his son, H A V Bulleid, recorded years later that his father was not greatly interested in the aesthetics of industrial design. Probably his most successful essay in this direction was his choice of bright malachite green as the Southern main-line locomotive livery. To some eyes even the Q1 was not out of the ordinary. The Bulleid family were having breakfast in their home adjacent to the line from Redhill to Reading outside London when the first Q1 passed the bottom of the garden. Everyone rushed out to see it, but the comment from the female side was that it was 'just an ordinary engine' – presumably no excuse for precipitate departure from the breakfast table.

Bulleid made another more radical break with steam locomotive convention in his 'Leader' class design of 1949. This was a steam equivalent of the power bogie electric locomotive except that the axles were not individually driven as in modern electric traction practice. The locomotive was carried on two three-axle bogies. In each of these bogies there was a

three-cylinder steam engine with sleeve-valve distribution driving the center axle; outer axles were coupled to the center axle by chain drives. There was a driver's cab at each end and a separate position for the fireman approximately at the middle of the locomotive as the boiler was off-center on the main frames and fired from the side. The discomfort of working in this position would have been serious, but could have been overcome for oil-firing. A more serious problem proved to be stretching of the chains and a consequent uneven distribution of the load between them (particularly when starting) which led to excessive wear. Work was put in hand on four locomotives of this type, but only one was completed and tested. The trials revealed too many problems to be overcome and the project was abandoned in 1951. The completed locomotive and those still under construction were scrapped.

Bulleid set out his philosophy of locomotive design in a paper written for the Institution of Mechanical Engineers entitled 'Stages in the Development of the Steam Locomotive to Restore It to Its Supremacy as the Ideal Railway Traction Unit.' The paper was never presented, at the request of British Railways, which was highly sensitive to criticism of spending money on experiments of doubtful value and by no means convinced that Bulleid's assessment of the status of the steam locomotive in railway traction was correct.

On the Great Western Railway, consideration of postwar requirements had revived the idea of a Great Western Pacific, and C B Collett's successor, F W Hawksworth, prepared a Pacific design using a 280 lb per square inch (19.7 kg/sq cm) boiler. No work on engines purely for express passenger traffic could be undertaken in the war years, but when, toward the end, the building of more mixed traffic locomotives was permitted Hawksworth introduced his 'County' class, a mixed-traffic 4—6—0 with the boiler pressure and wheel diameter (6 feet 3 inches/ 1905 mm) that had been proposed for the Pacific. The first of the series went into service in 1945. In the previous year Hawksworth had begun construction of a new batch of 'Hall' class 4—6—0s — the

Great Western's pioneer general purpose design — in which a higher degree of superheat was used. These 'modified Halls' continued the success of their predecessors in the new postwar environment.

After the war all the 'King' class locomotives on the Western Region were fitted with double blast-pipes and chimneys. Similar fitments were applied to new series of 'Castles' built in postwar years, and some of the earlier locomotives were similarly modified.

The first of the BR standard locomotive classes appeared in 1951. The 'Britannia Pacific' set the trend — it was a two-cylinder design with the emphasis on easy maintenance. The frames were massive, bearing surfaces of ample proportions and all running gear outside. Equipment included a self-cleaning smokebox, a rocking grate and hopper ashpan to lighten the tasks of the shed staff attending to the locomotive after its spell of duty. Self-cleaning devices had been fitted in some locomotive smokeboxes much earlier than this, but they were operated by the driver. During World War II certain locomotives were fitted with equipment which performed the function automatically and continuously. Wire mesh screens were fitted in the path of the gases from the fire where they emerged from the boiler tubes. These screens served to break down the larger cinders to a size which could be ejected through the chimney, instead of accumulating in the bottom of the smokebox to be cleared by the shed staff. Shed-staff duty was one of the less attractive aspects of attending to the steam locomotive and the railway companies were under no illusions about the difficulty of attracting labor to the railways. Railroad companies had to compete with newer industries which often offered less arduous working conditions. First experiments with the screens showed a detrimental effect on power obtained from the steam and it became evident that the insertion of these fittings in the smokebox made adjustments to the design and dimensions of blastpipe and chimney necessary. The lessons were learned and were applied to the design of the Standard classes.

The 'Britannia' Pacific, with 6-foot 2-inch (1880-mm) diameter wheels, was a general-purpose loco-

Far right: GW 'King' No 6010, *King Charles I*, pilots 'Britannia' No 70019, *Lightning*, on a down express near Aller Junction, where the Torquay branch diverges from the main line to Penzance.

Bottom: The 'basic steam locomotive,' exemplified by Bulleid Q1 class 0–6–0 No 33007 heading a ballast train. The class was introduced in 1942 and 40 were built.

Right: The last Great Western main-line locomotive design was F W Hawksworth's 'County' class 4–6–0, partly derived from a contemplated Pacific which was never built. No 1011, *County of Chester*, passes Bath with a Taunton–London (via Bristol) train on 11 August 1961.

motive. After some initial problems had been overcome it gave excellent service, even holding its own on express duties with other classes designed specifically for that type of work. The class first made its name on the completely recast and accelerated timetable between London, Norwich and other points in East Anglia, which was introduced soon after the new locomotives became available. A lighter version of the class with smaller cylinders was also built. During its short life the 'Britannia' was widely used in many parts of the BR system; migratory habits were forced upon it as more and more main-line diesels came into service.

Other classes in the first production of Standards were two 4–6–0s based on the celebrated LMS 'Black Five' of Stanier's day; a 2–6–4T also of LMS conception and a 2–6–2T based on a Great Western design. These were followed by three 2–6–0 mixed-traffic classes and a further 2–6–2T, but this time with LMS antecedents. The largest of the mixed-traffic 2–6–0s, with 5-foot 3-inch (1600-mm) coupled wheels and 225 lb per square inch (15.8 kg/sq cm) boiler pressure showed itself highly competent on light express duties on cross-country routes, with a good turn of speed.

High speeds with relatively small coupled wheels reflected the progress that had been made in improving the locomotive steam circuit and hence the ability to admit and exhaust steam adequately at high piston speeds. Perhaps the most remarkable demonstration of this capability was given by the last of the Standard classes to be produced in quantity, a 2–10–0 with 5-foot (1524-mm) coupled wheels intended for freight work plus general duties in the lower speed range. In practice these engines showed themselves capable of 90 mph (145 kph) on at least two well-attested occasions when put on to express passenger turns in an emergency.

The first of the 2–10–0s came out in 1954. A year later British Railways announced its Modernization Plan, one ingredient of which was the complete replacement of steam by diesel or electric traction. Despite the threat of extinction, however, efforts to improve the efficiency of steam traction continued, one of which was the building of ten of the 2–10–0s with Crosti boilers in 1955. The object of this type of boiler, used with some success in Italy and Germany, was to improve thermal efficiency by preheating the water fed into the boiler. The preheater was in effect a smaller boiler with flue tubes underneath the main boiler, into which the hot gases from the fire were directed on reaching the front smokebox. They then flowed back through the tubes in the preheater to a final smokebox at the firebox-end of the boiler, where they escaped to the atmosphere through a chimney. Exhaust steam from the cylinders was also piped back to the rear smokebox and expelled through the same chimney to create a draft, and a proportion passed through a jacket around the preheater to assist in raising the temperature of the feedwater by heat exchange. In British Rail locomotives the chimney was on the running plate on the right-hand side, adjacent to the firebox, but there was also a small chimney in the usual position on the front smokebox. This, however, was used only when lighting up the locomotive for initial steam-raising and was not in the exhaust steam circuit. All ten locomotives with Crosti boilers were eventually rebuilt with conventional exhaust arrangements.

Until World War II there had been only two

Above: A standard class 2 2–6–2T No 84005 leaves Manton Tunnel with the Stamford branch push-pull train on 3 April 1965. Left: A BR Standard class 4 4–6–0 No 75005 brings an unusual touch of modernity to the Cambrian section of the Western Region.

previous ten-coupled locomotives in Great Britain. The first had been a 0–10–0 tank engine built in 1903 by the Great Eastern Railway to demonstrate that a steam locomotive could accelerate a train as well as electric traction. The company was being pressed to electrify its London suburban services out of Liverpool Street and the slogan '30 mph in 30 seconds from rest' was the battle-cry of the campaign. The Great Eastern's 'Decapod' did even better with a load of about 280 US tons/250 UK tons/254 tonnes. Apparently the demonstration silenced the pressure group and the railway was saved from having to face the huge capital cost of electrification. Presumably this saving was compensation for the expense of building a locomotive which was of little practical use after having proved its point, for its weight, distributed over a wheelbase of only 19 feet 8 inches (5.9 m) was too great for the permanent way and it never went into regular service.

The Great Eastern continued to work its intensive suburban services with steam locomotives of more modest size, earning much admiration for its smart operating, notably the speed with which incoming trains were provided with new engines to take them out again, while engines which had just arrived were deftly dispatched to their next duties. Rush-hour signalling at Liverpool Street must have been an exhausting occupation, particularly in the days of hand-worked points and signals.

Above: Standard locomotives of power class 2 included a light 2–6–0 tender engine. No 78000, the first of the class, is at Shrewsbury in 1961.

Although the immediate demand for electrification had been silenced, however, it was revived from time to time and when government finance for new railway works was made available in the middle 1930s one of the approved schemes was the electrification of the line from Liverpool Street through the eastern suburbs of London to Shenfield in Essex, 20.25 miles (32.6 km). War postponed the work in 1939 and it was not completed until ten years later.

The second British ten-coupled locomotive was an 0–10–0 banking engine built by the Midland Railway for assisting trains on the Lickey Incline on its main line from Birmingham to Gloucester. It had a long and useful life and was still working in 1914 when a series of 2–10–0 locomotives was built by the North British Locomotive Company for the British War Department. It was the good performance of this class which led to the choice of the same wheel arrangement for the standard BR heavy freight locomotive – originally a 2–8–2 had been in mind. The last steam locomotive built for British Railways was one of the Standard 2–10–0s. It was named *Evening Star* and has been preserved in running order.

Although the 'Britannias' met most fast passenger train requirements on British Railways, the range of standard types was extended to include a design specifically made for express traffic. It was again a Pacific, but differed from all the others in that it had a three-cylinder engine. Wheel diameter was the same as in the 'Britannia' class, as this had been found satisfactory for free running at speeds up to 90 mph

(145 kph). The valve gear, however, was different from all the other standard engines, consisting of cam-operated poppet valves, and the locomotive was fitted with a double blastpipe. Only one engine was built to this design. Trials and service experience showed the need for some modifications on the steam-generating side, for the locomotive was less effective in this respect than the 'Britannias,' and relatively heavy on fuel. Already, however, the decision to abolish steam traction on British Railways had been taken and there was little incentive for further experiment and development of the design.

If its maximum steaming capacity was unimpressive, this Pacific, named *Duke of Gloucester*, was highly efficient in using what it did produce, improving by about 1 lb/ihp-hr on most contemporary simple-expansion designs and being bettered by the most advanced French compounds only to the same degree. Unfortunately it needed a different driving technique from the other Pacifics with which it was housed at Crewe North Motive Power Depot and, in the absence of a regular crew who could have learned its idiosyncracies, its performance did not do justice to its sophisticated design. It was withdrawn at the end of 1962 and its cylinders removed to be sectioned and displayed in the Science Museum in London. Over a decade later the other remains were rescued from a scrapyard in South Wales by a preservation society which began the formidable task of reconditioning it for a working life on a private railway.

In 1956, after the decree that steam was to be

phased out but before quantity production of main-line diesels had begun, there was a proposal to build more locomotives of the same class, and these would no doubt have improved on the original. However the plan did not materialize and the solitary *Duke* made its contribution to the last years of steam by providing information obtained from scientific testing of its performance on a stationary plant and on the road. As a result a similar poppet-valve gear was fitted to 30 BR standard class 5 locomotives built at Derby in 1956–57 and there were numerous applications of its double-exhaust system. Had steam survived, the influence of *Duke of Gloucester* would have been more durable.

Much was learned about the steam locomotive during its last years in Britain. World War II saw widespread development of measurement and recording systems, and of transducers for converting physical quantities into electrical signals. Locomotive testing went back many years, but these new scientific resources enabled it to be carried out on a greater scale and with more significant results. British Railways tested a number of the more recent locomotive classes and published bulletins giving findings that could have had a considerable effect on future design had steam locomotive building continued.

In earlier years one of the problems of locomotive testing on the road had been to find stretches of line where a locomotive could run in constant conditions long enough for useful measurements to be taken and without hindrance to other traffic. Early in the century Dr G V Lomonossoff had been a pioneer of locomotive testing in Russia, where long stretches of

level track with only light traffic could be found. The tests were considered to be of national importance and test trains were given the same priority as the Czar's own train. Similar advantages were not enjoyed elsewhere, and it was many years before a procedure was developed to obtain similar results without interfering with other traffic in Great Britain. This was the Controlled Road Testing System used on the Great Western Railway and the Western Region of British Railways. The essential feature of the system was measurement of the rate of steaming by detecting the fall of pressure across the blastpipe. A corresponding indication was given in the cab, and the driver held the instrument reading steady by adjustment of the cut-off, using the brakes to check speed when necessary, while the fireman maintained a constant rate of firing. In this way a test train could run at varying speeds without upsetting the measurements and could more easily be fitted into the timetable by the operating department. On the Great Western Railway these road tests supplemented tests on a stationary plant at Swindon. In 1939 a more advanced stationary installation for use by all the railways was being built at Rugby, but the work was held up by the war. After the war rehabilitation of the railways was given priority and the Rugby plant did not come into operation until 1950.

Although the end of steam had been decreed in the British Railways Modernization Plan in 1955, steam locomotives remained at work until August 1968. The effects of the new policy were barely noticeable until the early 1960s, when the pace of withdrawals accelerated. Early in 1961 there were still 241 loco-

Below: The 'Austerity' 2–10–0s built by the Ministry of Supply during the war were bought by British Railways. No 73788 is at the Rugby testing station in 1949, awaiting tests on the roller test plant. These locomotives led to the design of the 9F Standard 2–10–10s.

motives of the traditional British 4−4−0 wheel arrangement on the BR books, but all except one earmarked for preservation had been condemned by the end of 1962. Withdrawals then came so fast that they have been described as a 'massacre.' While lamented by enthusiasts, these events were little noticed by the travelling public at large who were more concerned at the shrinkage of the railway system itself under the proposals of a report, *The Re-shaping of British Railways*, prepared under the aegis of Dr (later Lord) Beeching, who became Chairman of the newly-formed British Railways Board on 1 January 1963. Rationalization weeded out or downgraded routes which had been built for competitive reasons but now simply duplicated facilities.

Surprisingly, the last London terminus to see main-line steam was Waterloo, Southern Region, which for many years had been the focus of an extensive electrified network. In the 1960s the Southern was busy completing electrification between Waterloo and the coastal resort of Bournemouth, and until this work was finished BR Standards and rebuilt Bulleid Pacifics continued to work the Bournemouth and Weymouth line trains. The end came on 8 July 1967 when 'West Country' Pacific No 34037, *Clovelly*, took the last steam-hauled passenger train out of the terminus on its way to Southampton Docks.

A dwindling band of steam locomotives carried on in northwest England until 11 August 1968. British Railways marked the end with a 'Last Day of Steam'

Below: Before the 'Austerities' and the 9Fs, the longest-lived British ten-coupled locomotive was the banking engine built by the Midland Railway for assisting trains on the Lickey Incline at Bromsgrove on the Derby–Bristol main line. In this view the banker, No 22290, is at Derby in LMS days after a major overhaul. Right: The only BR standard engine designed specifically for express traffic rather than general duties was No 71000, *Duke of Gloucester*. It was overtaken by the diesel program and withdrawn in 1962, but while at work contributed useful data under test which could have influenced future steam-locomotive design in Great Britain.

special from Liverpool to Carlisle and back. On the previous weekend enthusiasts' societies had chartered steam-hauled trains for commemorative trips from Birmingham to Huddersfield and from Manchester to Blackpool. Then, there was only the throb of the diesel or the hum of the traction motor through the length and breadth of British Railways.

Some would say that the world of steam is not quite lost, pointing to the achievements of the many preservation societies in reclaiming locomotives from the scrapyards and restoring them to running order to operate on lines long-since abandoned by British Railways. This is indeed a splendid and an international enterprise, and many barely of an age to remember the steam locomotive in its prime are ensnared by its fascination. What is more they pass on the same spirit to their children. Only the old and churlish occasionally prick the bubble by paraphrasing Marshal Bosquet's comment as he watched the Charge of the Light Brigade at Balaclava —

'C'est magnifique, mais ce n'est pas le chemin de fer.'

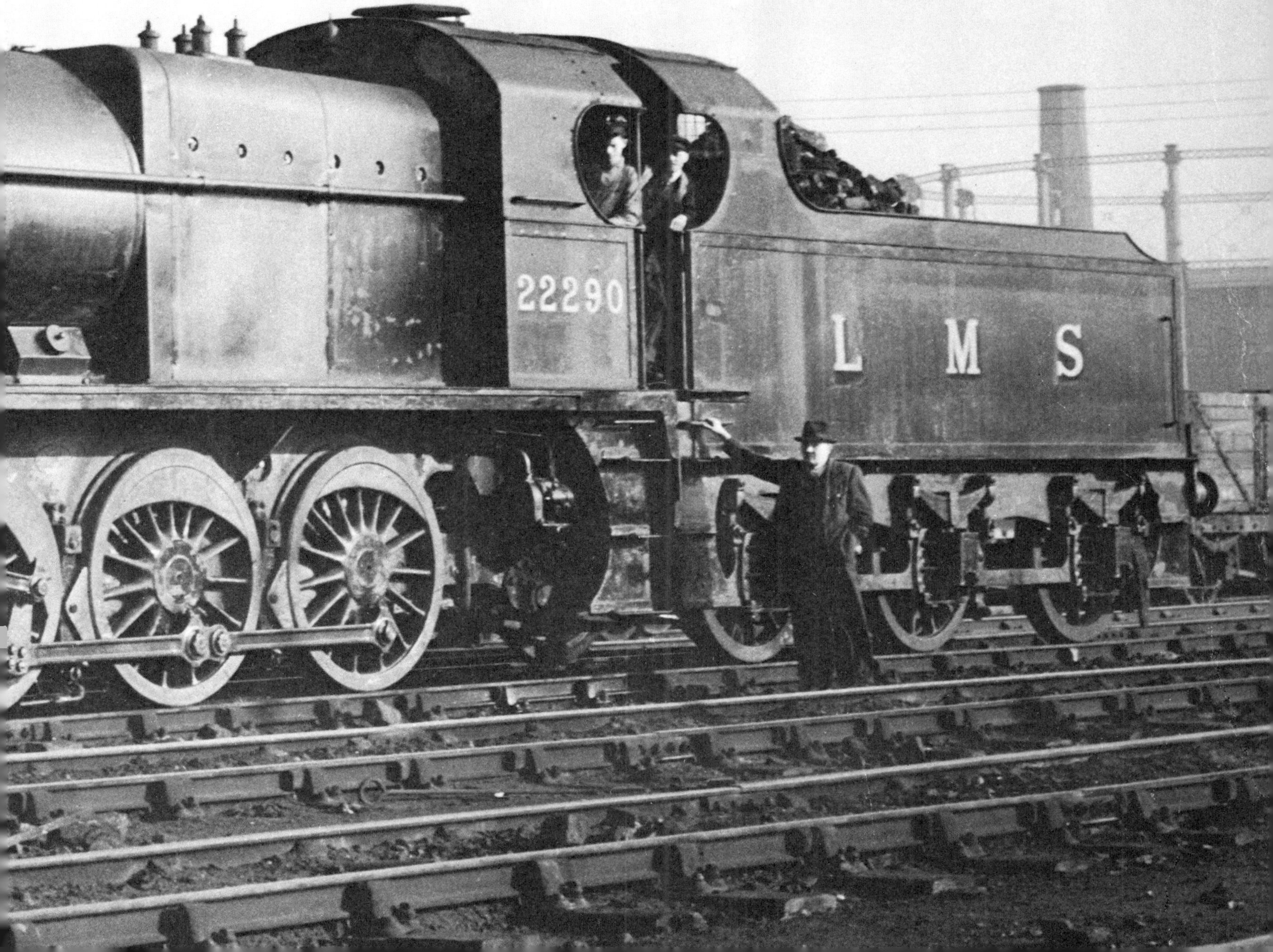

# 3. North American Steam

Though it was a British-made locomotive which was the first to run on an American railroad line, the development of railways in North America followed a very different pattern to that in Britain, just as the evolution of the locomotive turned the American versions into a distinctive creature well suited to the characteristics of the country.

Apart from the sheer size of the continent which required the building of lines over vast distances and adverse geological conditions, the railways of America were constructed under entirely different social conditions. In the 'old countries' railway companies found that their lines usually had to be built to fit into – or around – established communities and they became involved in complicated negotiations over land rights. In North America there were considerably fewer long-established communities and there were vast tracts of land on which there were no rights of ownership. In the old world the railroads were used to connect existing towns and cities; in America the railroads were not only a means of communication between communities but also served to open up the country and actually attracted the development of new settlements.

The historic first run by a locomotive in the USA was made by Horatio Allen of the Delaware and Hudson Canal Company on board the *Stourbridge Lion* which had been built for Allen by Foster, Rastrick

& Company of Stourbridge, England to operate on a 16-mile (25.7-km) line between Carbondale coal mines and the canal at Honesdale, Pennsylvania. Allen, who had never driven a locomotive before, confessed later to having been fearful of making that first run and in fact insisted that he make it alone on the basis that 'If there is any danger on this ride it is not necessary that the life and limb of more than one be subjected to danger.' The journey of three miles (4.8 km) was completed successfully but neither the *Lion* nor the *America*, which had been ordered from Robert Stephenson & Company together, proved suitable for the track and were taken out of service.

The real development of railways in the early days of steam locomotion in the United States was undertaken by the Baltimore & Ohio Railroad and the South Carolina Railroad. The latter was the first passenger line in America, and second in the world to the British Liverpool and Manchester line, to rely entirely on steam locomotion. However, it was on the former that steam locomotion in North America really began, although when the line was inaugurated in 1829 it was built to use horse traction. When Peter Cooper of New York demonstrated his *Tom Thumb* vertical-boilered engine to the directors, they were sufficiently impressed to organize a locomotive competition, similar to the famous 'Rainhill trials' held in England in 1829.

Right: The Santa Fe Express halts at Virginia City in 1885, headed by Virginia & Truckee 4–4–0 No 11, *Rene*.
Below left: 'American' 4–4–0s at a busy junction in New York State are depicted in an engraving of 1874. The vehicle on the extreme right is a 'Pullman Palace Drawing Room and Sleeping Car.'
Below: An impression of a train on the Hudson River Railroad (later absorbed into the New York Central & Hudson River) shows the ornamentation of locomotives that was practiced in the nineteenth century and the prevalence of bogie vehicles at a period when British travellers generally rode on six wheels.
Below right: Shunting at a yard on the Central Pacific Railroad about 1869. The site is probably near Salt Lake City, Utah.

**'Don't let the studio guys dictate to you. They want to take you over . . . mould you'**

*Unlucky in love: (left) Marilyn in 1954, shortly before she made 'The Seven-Year Itch' and already twice married; (inset) in 1953 'How to Marry a Millionaire'*

# What the banks giveth, the banks taketh away.

After years of raking in the interest on current accounts, four of the High Street banks have announced that they are going to return this interest to its rightful owners: their customers.

They have been forced to change their policy for a simple but compelling reason.

Their customers are deserting them by the thousands in favour of

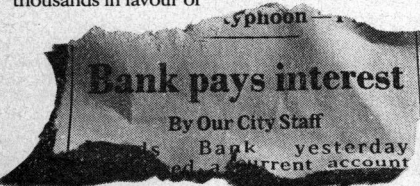

**Bank pays interest**

By Our City Staff

Nationwide Anglia's FlexAccount.

Which is understandable.

After all, a FlexAccount is a current account that earns interest as soon as the first £1 enters the account. And goes on earning it all the time your account is in the black.

No ifs. No buts. Indeed, no wrinkles of any kind whatsoever.

And unlike the banks, we don't have all sorts of different current accounts, only some of which pay you interest.

At Nationwide Anglia, you don't have to ask for interest on your money: *all* FlexAccount holders receive it automatically.

And while the interest is paid annually, it's calculated daily. So the minute your salary comes in, it starts making you money.

Even though some of the banks' new current accounts are copying one aspect of FlexAccount by giving you interest, most banks still haven't changed their attitude to charges.

In fact, according to the publicity blurb,

practically all of the new interest-bearing current accounts have charges which are even higher than they were before.

For instance, go more than £100 overdrawn with one of these new bank current accounts even with their permission, and you'll be landed with a charge of £6 per month.

For what? Your guess is as good as ours.

MONTHLY FEE

Another of these new accounts has a fixed £10 monthly charge just for the privilege of having the account.

As you might expect, at Nationwide Anglia our attitude is somewhat different.

With a FlexAccount, there are no transaction charges or fixed fees of any kind.

Even when you go into the red.

No overdraft administration charge. No maintenance charge. No service charge.

If you want to arrange an overdraft we'll get together with you and discuss the subject in a sensible manner.

Then all we ask is interest on the money outstanding for however many days your account is overdrawn.

Simple. Understandable. And, hopefully, fair.

Indeed, it is easy to understand why in just eighteen months over one million people have opened FlexAccounts.

Particularly when you consider all the other facilities it offers.

Obviously, there are cheque books, cheque guarantee cards and cash cards. Not to mention other services like standing orders, direct debits, bill payments and 24-hour cash dispensers.

FlexAccount holders have also enjoyed something they've had great difficulty getting from banks.

An open, honest, adult relationship which respects the fact that it is your money, not ours.

The banks may think that by copying our ideas they can win back their customers.

But do you know something?

They can borrow the ideas, but they'll never be able to steal the philosophy.

For more information call in to your local Nationwide Anglia Building Society branch. Or write today to Claire Adams at Nationwide Anglia Building Society, Chesterfield House, Bloomsbury Way, London WC1V 6PW.

**Nationwide Anglia** Building Society

**FlexAccount. We always remember whose money it is.**

FP2

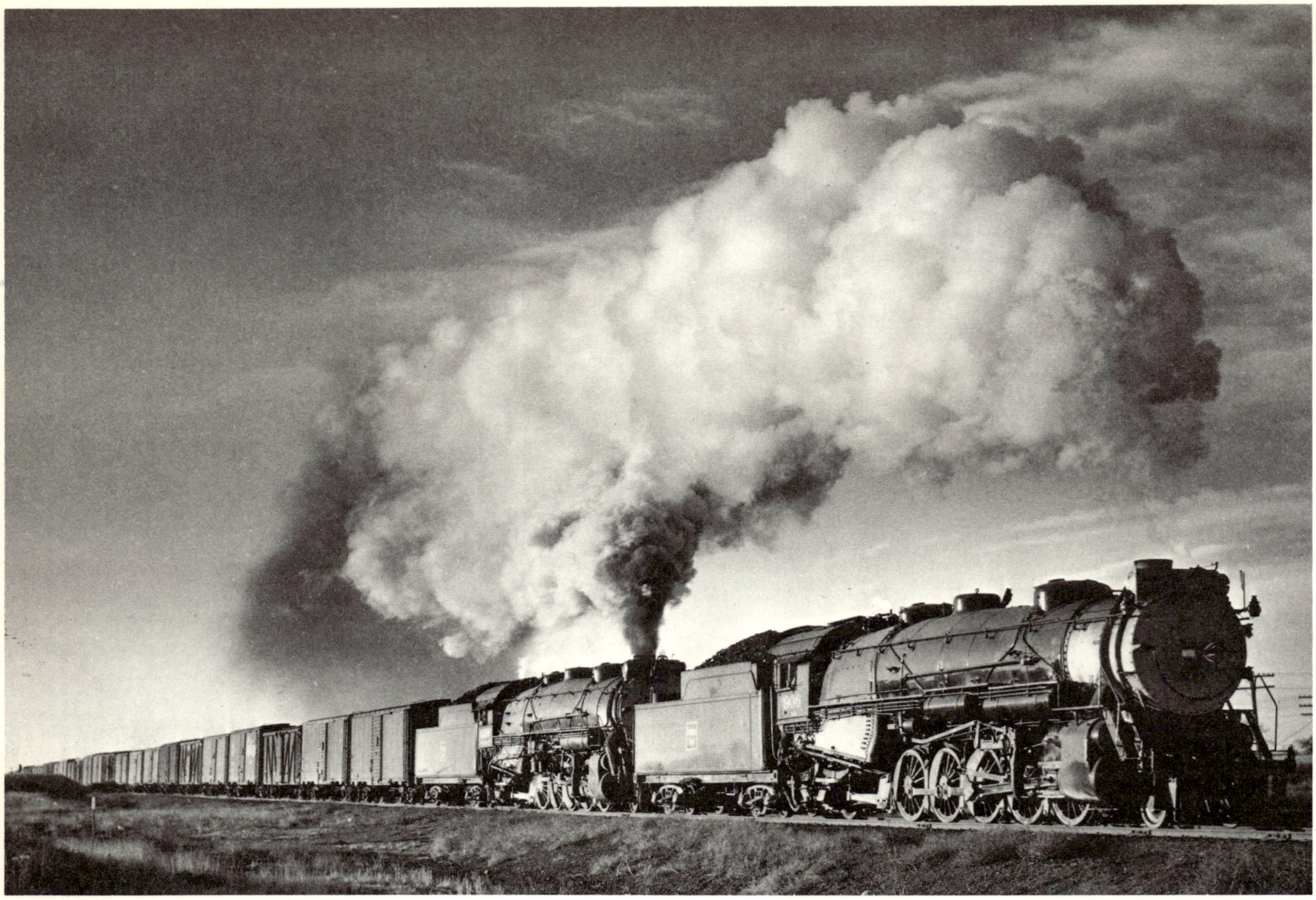

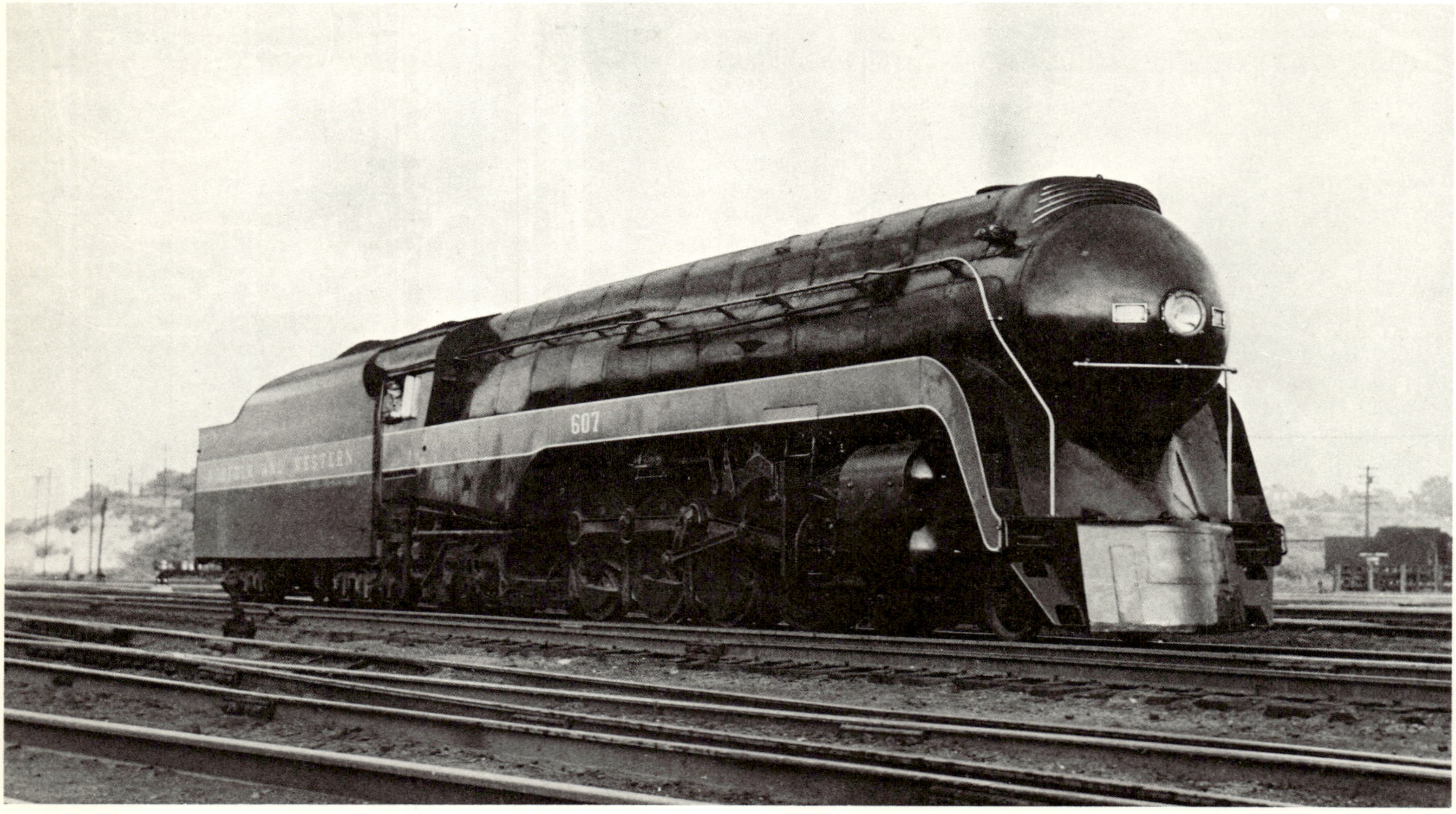
607

Above: A New York Central
Hudson (4–6–4) cautiously
approaches a maze of
crossings.
Top left: Two 2–10–2 locomotives of the standard
gauge Colorado & Southern
leave Denver, Colorado,
with a freight for Cheyenne,
Wyoming.
Left: Streamlined 4–8–4
No 607 of the Norfolk &
Western Railroad is typical
of the cleaner lines achieved
in US locomotive design
toward the end of steam.

The Baltimore trials in 1831 had a more practical basis than those at Rainhill. Rather than a straight-forward speed test the American contestants were required to submit their locomotives to a month's service hauling traffic. From the five entrants the vertical boiler *York*, designed by Phineas Davies, a watchmaker, was judged the winner of the $4000 first prize and the locomotive became the prototype for a fleet of 18 engines, the last of which did not retire until 1893 and was the oldest working loco-motive in the world at that time.

The success of the Baltimore & Ohio and the South Carolina Railroads led to a burst of activity; a host of new companies sprung up to thrust out lines into the virgin lands of North America. While British railway builders may have been staggered by the enormity of the task of building railroads in North America they might also have been horrified by the standard of construction. In Britain and Europe lines were robustly built to careful specifications but in North America the keynote was speed and cheapness. The rush was on to open up the country as quickly as possible and only when lines had proved them-selves economically viable were improvements made to the original, often dangerously flimsy, construc-tions. The hasty and haphazard approach by so many independent companies led to a complete lack of standardization in gauges. Many early lines in the northern states were built to a 3-foot (914-mm) gauge, while the southern states adopted South Carolina's 5-foot (1524-mm) gauge and the Erie

Railroad of 1841 was started with a gauge of 6 feet (1829 mm). Eventually, when the first transconti-nental railroad came to be built, Congress approved a standard gauge of 4 feet 8.5 inches (1435 mm). Such was the rate of construction that even by 1835 railroads in the Eastern States accounted for more than half the world's total track length of 1600 miles (2575 km).

The idea of a transcontinental railroad had been the dream of pioneers and a few impractical theorists since early in the century but it became a political and economic necessity with the rapid population growth in the West coupled with the discovery of gold in the 1840s. Even then the political and commercial maneuverings rumbled on for years while rival factions suggested various routes and schemes, fre-quently without the backing of accurate surveys. Finally the Senate passed the Pacific Railroad Act in June 1862, granting two charters: one to the Union Pacific to build west from a suitable terminus in the center of the continent and the other to the Central Pacific Railroad to build east from Sacramento. The following year Union Pacific began building from Omaha, Nebraska and Central Pacific from Sacra-mento. The two lines eventually met at Promontory in May 1869. Over the years other companies com-pleted their transcontinental lines — the Atchison Topeka & Santa Fé, the Southern Pacific, the Northern Pacific and the Chicago, Milwaukee, St Paul & Pacific — but their histories are well documented elsewhere.

The golden age of steam for the United States was

in the early years of this century. By this time the worst features of 'jerrybuilding' had been corrected, routes improved and locomotives of juggernaut proportions had evolved into what was to be their final form. Valves had changed from the 'flat-iron' slide version to less friction-bound piston types; fireboxes had deepened to give more heat and hence more power.

It was this big grate which was to give the world a new railroad language. The deep fireboxes left no room for driving wheels underneath and so small carrying wheels on a pony truck at the rear were added to the guiding wheels on a front truck to provide the common wheel arrangements which became a worldwide method of identification associated forever with the names of the types which first carried them. Hence we had the 4–4–2 Atlantics, the 4–6–2 Pacifics, the 2–6–2 Prairies and the less widely known 2–8–2 Mikados, which, with the Pacifics, became the standard freight locomotives in the United States for over 20 years. Those names were a reference to the first orders for the locomotives:

Right: The 'Hiawatha' with a Hudson at the head runs through the outskirts of Chicago at the start of its 410-mile journey to St Paul.

Left: Ready for the return trip to Chicago, the 'Hiawatha's' Hudson waits with its train for the rightaway from St Paul.
Below: A Chicago & North Western streamlined Hudson locomotive pauses at Cedar Rapids, Iowa, with the eastbound Pacific Limited (Los Angeles–Chicago). These engines performed briefly on the 400 (Chicago–St Paul) express but were superseded after a year by diesels.
Below right: One of the streamlined Atlantics built for the 'Hiawatha' express sets out on the high-speed run with its train of matching coaches.

the first 4—6—2 crossed the Pacific to New Zealand, the first 2—8—2 went to Japan and the first 4—4—2 was ordered by the Atlantic Coast line.

Enlargement of the grate obviously meant that larger stocks of coal had to be carried, to the extent that it was sometimes impossible for the fireman to keep up with the demands of the firebox. The answer was automatic stoking. A screw-feed mechanism powered by a small steam donkey engine became the most usual method, the coal being distributed evenly within the grate by jets of steam.

By the end of World War I North America had 72,000 working locomotives. Thereafter the number began, slowly, to decline but improvements in details of design continued to meet demands of speed and higher performance standards. One of the major alterations involved adding extra driving wheels while another involved articulation, which called for even more wheels! This 'stretching' of locomotives led to the giant locomotives with eight-coupled driving wheels for passenger work and ten or 12 for freight work. The ultimate was the 4—8—8—4 'Big Boy,' first produced for Union Pacific in 1941 for freight service. We shall return to this later.

Although the locomotives of North America had, like all others, evolved directly from Stephenson's *Rocket*, their appearance by the end of World War I was a clear indication of the different line of evolution which North American designers had taken to that of their British and European cousins. However, British design *did* have some influence on the external appearance of many locomotives after 1927. It was in that year that the famous British 4—6—0 of the Great Western Railway, *King George V*, visited North America and left a lasting impression for its clean lines. Thereafter there was a determined effort on the part of many railroads to conceal the extraneous pipework of their locomotives under boilerjackets and generally to smooth down and improve their external appearance. The end result tended to be a cleaner-looking breed of locomotive which, nonetheless, retained its distinctive workman-like appearance.

The coming of the 1930s saw the introduction of the great steam-hauled express trains of North America. Chicago & North Western announced that it was going to launch an express that would cover the 408.6 miles (657.6 km) between Chicago and St Paul in seven hours, cutting the previous best time by 170 minutes. The new train, called the '400,' first ran on 6 January 1935. Over the 209.5 miles (337.2 km) from Chicago to Adams the train had to average 63.8 mph (102.7 kph) to the first stop at Milwaukee, 85 miles (136.8 km) from Chicago, and then cover the remaining distance to Adams at the same average speed. In its early days the train was formed of five air-conditioned steel coaches headed by an oil-burning Pacific locomotive which had been modified for the service by the substitution of 6-foot 7-inch diameter (2007-mm) driving wheels for those of 6-foot 3-inch (1905-mm) diameter originally fitted. The '400' triggered a railway 'race' between Chicago and the Twin Cities of St Paul and Minneapolis.

This was a less well-known but more significant phase in railway history than the railway races in Great Britain from London to Edinburgh and to Aberdeen in the previous century. It is true that the earlier British events had a commercial motive in that the company making the fastest run would gain prestige, but to the ordinary traveller the frequent changes in schedules must have been irritating, while the 'racing' trains often landed him at his destination at an inconveniently early hour. Moreover, the companies involved were unlikely to make their best performance the standard for everyday running in future. On the other hand the schedules of the American expresses were a regular offer and planned for the convenience of the railway customer.

The other line using steam traction between Chicago and the Twin Cities was the Chicago, Milwaukee, St Paul and Pacific, which, not unreasonably, preferred to call itself in its publicity simply 'The Milwaukee Road.' Response from this quarter to the '400' was swift. A new service called the 'Hiawatha' was scheduled to run from Chicago to St Paul in 6.5 hours for the journey by this route of 410.5 miles (660.6 km), with four intermediate

stops. The 'Hiawatha' service was introduced on 29 May 1935 and immediately attracted attention by a very fast start-to-stop timing – 62 minutes for the 78.3 miles (126 km) from Sparta to Portage, representing an average of 75.8 mph (121.9 kph) and the fastest steam run in the world at that time.

The Chicago & North Western's '400' was not a streamliner. Locomotives and coaches were of conventional outline and the locomotives were normal members of their class except for the larger driving wheels already mentioned. For the 'Hiawatha,' however, new streamlined locomotives and coaches were built. The American Locomotive Company at Schenectady built two Atlantics for the service in 1934, and added two more shortly afterward. The engines had the high working pressure of 300 lb per square inch (21.1 kg/sq cm) and driving wheels of 7 feet (2134 mm) diameter. Oil-firing was chosen because it was feared that on a long high-speed run of over 400 miles (643 km) the ash accumulation would be excessive. Two outside cylinders drove the leading pair of coupled wheels, which was unusual in American Atlantics, but in other respects the engines were in line with well-established design practice.

The first streamlined 'Hiawatha' trains were six-car formations weighing 351 US tons/313 UK tons/318 tonnes and seating 376 passengers. In 1938 new stock was introduced and normally formed into nine-car trains weighing 482 US tons/430 UK tons/437 tonnes with seating for 499. Each train comprised a combined baggage and buffet car, four luxury cars for 'coach' class passengers (equivalent to second class), a café-dining car, two parlor cars and a parlor observation car. The last-named had a 'beaver tail' end and a somewhat unusual array of fins which served both to shield the rear windows from the sun and to strengthen the car at the back against the effects of possible impact. Special attention was paid to the suspension system so that shocks were absorbed and vibration suppressed.

From 1935 to 1939 there was one 'Hiawatha' train in each direction, both leaving the respective terminals at 1 pm. From 21 January 1939 an additional morning service was introduced and by that

Right: Closeup of a Pennsylvania T–1 4–4–4–4 showing the characteristic Raymond Loewy style of streamlining and the 16-wheel tender.
Below: A Pennsylvania Railroad K4 Pacific assists one of the T–1 class 4–4–4–4s with a heavy train on the Horseshoe Curve.

time the popularity of the train had grown to the extent that sometimes 15 cars had to be run. To meet these developments the railway commissioned six more powerful locomotives of the 4–6–4 wheel arrangement and put them into traffic in 1938. These were the new F7 class Hudsons, which became among the United States' finest locomotives. Normally they worked the morning 'Hiawathas' – the midday trains continued to run with the original Atlantics. From 28 January 1940, when the services were accelerated, one of the 4–6–4s had the task of making the Sparta–Portage run with the eastbound morning 'Hiawatha' in only 59 minutes, giving an average speed of 79.6 mph (128.1 kph) which put it far ahead of any contemporary steam competitor.

The 4–6–4s were coal-fired with automatic stokers. Boiler pressure and wheel diameter were the same as in the Atlantics. Diesels began to appear on the 'Hiawatha' in 1941, by which time the speed over the fastest stretch had been raised to 81 mph (130 kph). Perhaps spurred by diesel competition, the 4–6–4s now gave some of their best performances. They could, and did, sustain a speed of 100 mph (161 kph) over long distances with loads of 784 US tons/700 UK tons/711 tonnes. On one occasion an engine of this class hauling 874 US tons/780 UK tons/792.9 tonnes averaged 100.5 mph (161.7 kph) for 62 miles (99.8 km) continuously. In spite of these performances, the engine crews preferred the Atlantics, which gave them a smoother ride, and these locomotives continued to work on the service when loads did not exceed nine cars. During the war years, the use of diesels increased, although steam continued to share the work until 1945. Thereafter the Atlantics and Hudsons appeared in emergencies only and all engines of both classes had gone by 1951.

Nine streamlined 4–6–4s were built for the Chicago & North Western in 1938 to take over the '400' from the original Pacifics but a year later this train became regularly diesel-hauled. Like both classes of high-speed engines on the Milwaukee, the C&NW had 7-foot (2134-mm) diameter driving wheels.

The revival of the Atlantics for high-speed service in the USA and in Belgium aroused considerable

Right: T–1 4–4–4–4 No 5537 leaves Fort Wayne with the Pennsylvania's 'Fast Mail.'

Below: A Southern Pacific streamlined 4–8–4 of class GS3, in distinctive livery to match the coaches of the 'Daylight' express behind its tender, on its journey from Los Angeles to San Francisco.

Bottom: The Pennsylvania adopted the 'duplex' arrangement of the T–1s for freight service as well, building first a 4–6–4–4 design (class Q–1) and then a 4–4–6–4 here. These 26 engines formed class Q–2.

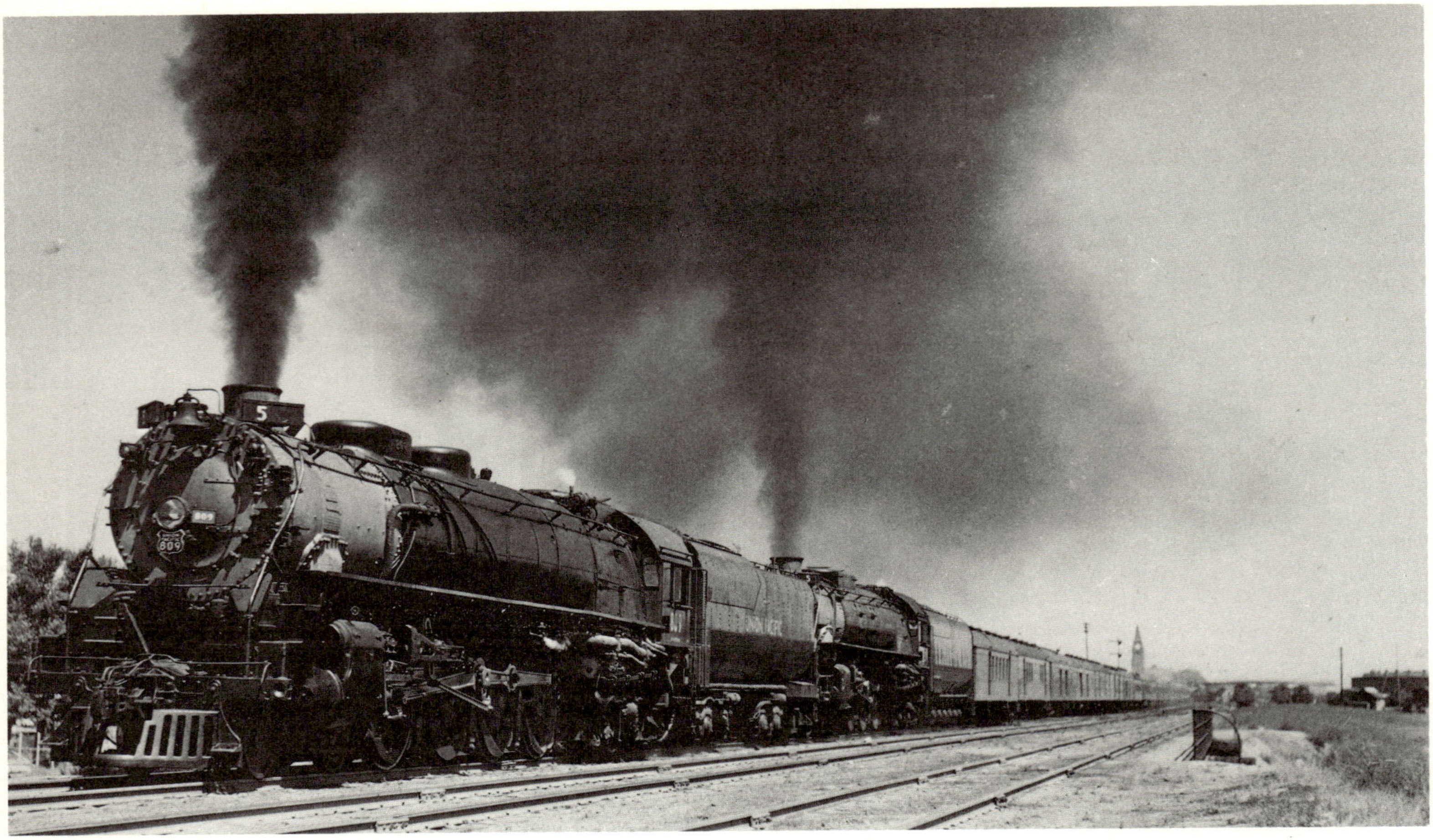
5
809

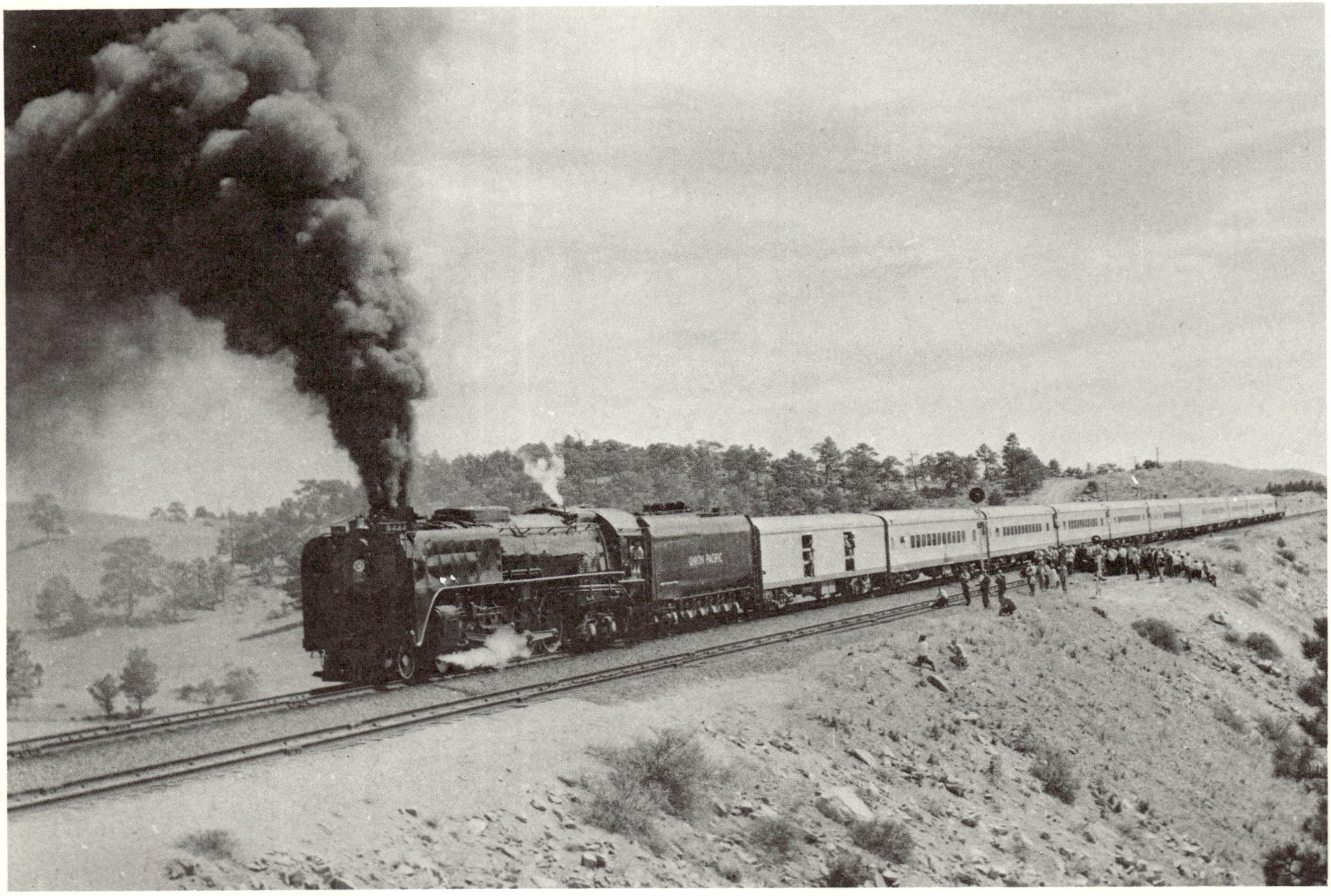

comment at the time, but it is less well known that older locomotives of this wheel arrangement also figured in the general speed-up in the 1930s. When the 'Hiawatha' was introduced, the 'Detroit Arrow' of the Pennsylvania Railroad, a Chicago—Detroit Service, was already covering the 64.2 miles (103.3 km) from Plymouth to Fort Wayne in 51 minutes, achieving an average speed of 75.5 mph (121.5 kph) and the locomotives used at first were Pennsylvania Atlantics dating from 1915. In Europe the Paris, Lyons & Mediterranean Railway in 1935 rebuilt an even older Atlantic, dating from 1906–07, for working an experimental streamlined train between Paris and Lyons. At that period the speed limit in France was 75 mph (120 kph) but on a trial run the streamlined four-cylinder compound hauling three coaches and a dynamometer car reached 97 mph (156 kph).

One of the best known 'families' of Hudsons ran on the New York Central, where the 1930s saw accelerations of long-established trains which were as demanding on the steam locomotive as the new high-speed services. There were several series of NYC Hudsons, going back to 1927. The earlier types were classified J–1a to J–1e; all had certain differences of detail but common features included two outside cylinders, 25 by 28 inches (635 by 711 mm), 6-foot 7-inch (2007-mm) diameter coupled wheels, 225 lb per square inch (15.8 kg/sq cm) boiler pressure, and a booster driving the rear axle of the training truck. Because of the booster, the diameter of the rear wheels in the truck, 4 feet 3 inches (1295 mm), was greater than that of the leading pair, 3 feet (914 mm).

All these locomotives performed well on heavy trains at high speeds and were associated in particular with the crack New York—Chicago express, the 'Twentieth Century Limited,' on which they began to replace Pacifics from 1927. When the J–1e series came out in 1932 the previous 20-hour schedule of this train had been cut to 18 hours for the 926 miles (1490.2 km). The train left Grand Central Terminal, New York, behind an electric locomotive and steam took over at Harmon, 33 miles (53.1 km) out. At Syracuse it ran for 1.3 miles (2.1 km) along a main thoroughfare, Washington Street, the locomotive bell tolling continuously. This procedure continued until the street section was by-passed in 1936, when the journey time was reduced to 16.5 hours, including seven intermediate stops.

The railway travel market in the 1930s was demanding. To meet growing expectations for comfort and service, operators called for new rolling stock which imposed an extra load on the locomotives not only in increased weight but also in power required for air-conditioning and other electrically based amenities. A more powerful version of the Hudson type had been planned as early as 1931. It materialized in 40 locomotives delivered by the American Locomotive Company (Alco) late in 1937, forming the J–3a series. The engines had a new boiler of greater evaporative capacity, working at 275 lb per square inch (19.3 kg/ sq cm), although this was later reduced to 265 lb per square inch (18.6 kg/sq cm). Cylinder dimensions were changed as well to 22.5 by 29 inches (571 by 737 mm). The first 40 engines were followed in 1938 by ten of a streamlined version.

These were not the first NYC streamliners, however. Responding to the growing fashion of the day, one of the J–1e series had been streamlined in 1934 and named *Commodore Vanderbilt*. It was often to be seen on the famous 'Twentieth Century Limited' between Chicago and Toledo, a run of 233 miles (375 km). Toledo was a locomotive changing point; changes were also made at Harmon (from electric traction as already noted) and Buffalo. Trains calling at Cleveland, where reversal was necessary in the Union Terminal station, also changed engines there, but the terminal could be by-passed and the 'Twentieth Century Limited' did not call there after the 1920s. In the later Hudsons some of the changes were omitted and the engines made very long through-runs such as from Harmon to Toledo, 693 miles (1115.3 km); or right through from Harmon to Chicago, 925 miles (1488.6 km).

The style of streamlining chosen for the J–3a engines was different from that originally adopted for *Commodore Vanderbilt* and soon became the accepted public image of the New York Central. In 1939 *Commodore Vanderbilt* was reclad in the new style. Two more of the J–3a series were streamlined for working the 'Empire State Express' after it acquired new stainless-steel stock. With the introduction of the J–3a engines the timing of the 'Twentieth Century Limited' was reduced to 16 hours, and it remained thus until the United States entered World War II in December 1941. With the return of peacetime conditions the schedule was resumed, but was cut to 15.5 hours from 1 April 1947. In the immediate postwar period the Hudsons yielded their heavier duties to new 4—8—4s but steam was nearing its end and by the time of the 1947 acceleration, multiple-unit diesel locomotives were becoming the normal power for the 'Twentieth Century Limited.' This famous express ceased to run on 13 March 1967 in the twilight of the long-distance American express passenger train.

The rival of the 'Twentieth Century Limited' for the New York—Chicago traffic was the 'Broadway Limited' of the Pennsylvania Railroad. This company had electrified its main line from New York to Philadelphia and Washington in 1933 and, with further electrification in mind, was not actively engaged in developing new steam locomotive designs. Its staple main-line power up to World War II consisted of a series of Pacifics of a class first seen in a single example in 1914. Series production began three years later and continued until 1928, by which time 425 had been built, including the prototype. The whole series was classified K4. There were differences between various production models but basically the locomotive was a two-cylinder simple with cylinders 27 by 28 inches (686 by 711 mm), 205 lb per square inch (14.4 kg/ sq cm) boiler pressure, and 6-foot 8-inch (2032-mm) diameter coupled wheels. Walschaerts valve gear was fitted to all engines as built but there were later experiments with poppet valves when double-heading was found necessary on the fastest and heaviest trains. Tests showed that the existing steam circuit would not meet the requirement of 100 mph (161 kph) on the level with 1000 US tons/893 UK tons/907 tonnes – the standard being sought by the Association of American Railroads.

No further development of the class took place, however, for the Pennsylvania decided to go in a completely new direction. In 1929–30, on the threshold of the speed and load revolution, two slightly larger Pacifics known as Class K5 were built but there was no follow-up here either. They are proof that the Locomotive Department was looking ahead even though the management may have been

Left: CNR streamlined
4–8–4 No 6401 at work on
a Toronto–Windsor service.

Below: A rebuilt 4–8–4 of
the Canadian National
passes Lachine with the
Ottawan evening business
express from Montreal.

Above: A Canadian
National 4–8–4 on the
turntable at Glen Yards,
Montreal.

inhibited from further investment in steam locomotives by thoughts of future electrification.

By the late 1930s there was a sudden change. Electrification extensions were only a long-term prospect and discussions took place with locomotive manufacturers on how best to meet current needs. It was decided that the answer would be a 'duplex' locomotive of the type favored by the Baldwin Locomotive Works. Essentially a 'duplex' meant having two two-cylinder steam engines in one nonarticulated frame, each pair of cylinders driving its own set of coupled wheels.

The first Pennsylvania 'duplex' was the one and only locomotive of the S–1 class, the largest rigid frame passenger locomotive ever built. Wheel arrangement was 6–4–4–6, the six-wheel bogies fore and aft being necessary to share in the support of a boiler no less than 62 feet 4 inches (18.9 m) long from firebox backplate to smokebox door. The diameter of the leading bogie wheels was 3 feet 6 inches (1118 mm), and that of the trailing wheels 4 feet 2 inches (1270 mm). Coupled wheel diameter was 7 feet (2134 mm) and the rigid driving wheelbase 64 feet 4 inches (19.6 m). A 16-wheel double-bogie tender contributed to an overall length of the whole locomotive of 140 feet 2.5 inches (42.7 m).

This gigantic locomotive ran on the main line only briefly before being put on exhibition at the New York World Fair in 1939 where it was the centerpiece of a joint 'American Railroad' display. Nearly a year

Below: Somewhat naturally the big coal-carrying road, the Norfolk & Western, was one of the last North American railroads to use steam. Its engines as well as its trains were huge and heavy, like this 2–8–8–2 at Shenendoah, Virginia, in 1956.

Right: The Union Pacific has left one of its last-built express steam locomotives for use on fan specials. This loco, No 8444, a massive 4–8–4 with headlights aglow takes a special Centennial excursion from Salt Lake City to Ogden and back.

Bottom: Another Norfolk & Western giant, this time a class A 2–6–6–4, heads a passenger train eastbound near River Gorge, Ripplemead, Virginia.

later it went into service on the Chicago–New York main line but was restricted by its weight to the section between Chicago and Crestline, 283 miles (455.4 km) long. Here it worked the principal trains and could average 66 mph (106 kph) westbound or 63 mph (101 kph) eastbound with a load of 1350 US tons/1205 UK tons/1224 tonnes, reaching 100 mph (161 kph) on slight downgrades. But its appetite for fuel was voracious; it was retired from active service about 1944 and scrapped in 1949.

If not wholly satisfied with its first essay in the duplex field, the Pennsylvania nonetheless went ahead with the principle and in 1940 ordered two 4–4–4–4s, built to more modest dimensions than the S–1 prototype but again with a boiler pressure of 300 lb per square inch (21.1 kg/sq cm). Coupled wheel diameter was slightly less at 6 feet 8 inches (2032 mm). These were followed in 1945 by 50 production engines, sufficiently similar to the first two for the whole series to be classified T–1. The external 'air-smoothed' design was created by Raymond Loewy, who had also been responsible for the S–1, but in the 4–4–4–4s he substituted a jutting 'prow' for the bulbous contours of the earlier design, foreshadowing the 'nose' of later diesels. Various changes in the shaping and extent of the exterior casing took place during the life of the locomotives.

**Right: Two CNR 4–8–4s at rest in Brockville Yard, Ontario. No 6258, on the right, worked the Royal Train in Canada in 1938 and carries a special plate below the headlight.**
**Below: Dormant power at Sherbrooke, Quebec, as a CNR Pacific waits to leave with a night train for Montreal.**

Below: One of the Norfolk & Western's magnificent class J streamlined 4–8–4s with a westbound passenger train at Bluefield.
Left: Pennsylvania Railroad 2–10–0s descending the Horseshoe Curve, Altoona, Pennsylvania, after banking a heavy freight.
Below left: Big Boy: the Union Pacifics giant at rest at Steamtown Museum, Bellows Falls.

The T—1s worked as far east as Harrisburg on the Chicago—New York main line and worked on all the crack trains, some of them making start-to-stop runs of between 120 and 140 miles (193 and 225 km) at speeds over 70 mph (113 kph). On many occasions they were recorded as running at 100 mph (161 kph) with a load of 1000 US tons/893 UK tons/907 tonnes. However, they were heavy on fuel and overshadowed from the first by the challenge of the diesel. By 1949 most of them had been retired. Scrapping began in 1951.

Duplex locomotives were also built for fast freight work on the Pennsylvania in the 1940s; the first was a 4—6—4—4 completed in 1942. In this prototype design, class Q—1, the first three-coupled axles were driven by cylinders in the usual position under the smokebox, but the cylinders for the rear pair were behind them, below the firebox and drove 'forward.' It was not a satisfactory arrangement because of heat, abrasive dirt, awkward steampipe connections and poor support for the slidebars. Surprisingly in a freight locomotive, the coupled wheel diameter was 6 feet 5 inches (1956 mm). The next move was to a freight duplex production series, class Q—2. Here the wheel arrangement was reversed; the four-coupled engine was in the front and the six-coupler at the rear. The coupled wheel diameter of this 4—4—6—4 was reduced to 5 feet 9 inches (1753 mm). The second pair of cylinders was arranged in front of its coupled axle group in the usual way. Deliveries of 26 Q—2 class locomotives were made in 1944 and 1945. Some of them outlived the T—1 passenger engines, continuing to work until 1951, but the Pennsylvania's leap forward from conventional Pacifics to the duplex system could not be judged a success by any standards.

In seeking higher power many railways in North America chose the 4—8—4 wheel arrangement. The name 'Niagara' adopted for this type of locomotive by the New York Central did not enjoy general usage. It has been mentioned already that the NYC began replacing its Hudsons with 4—8—4s in the mid-1940s, but there were many earlier examples. The Southern Pacific introduced eight classes between 1930 and 1943, all oil-fired and with boosters. Best remembered of them is class GS3 ordered in 1937 for working the 'Daylight' express (San Francisco—Los Angeles), the first of five classes with 6-foot 8-inch (2032-mm) diameter driving wheels. When inaugurated in the 1920s the 'Daylight' was allowed 12 hours for its journey of 471 miles (758 km), which abounded in long gradients of 1-in-100, short stretches as steep as 1-in-46, and severe curvatures. The new motive power was needed for an accelerated schedule in 1938 which cut the time to 9 hours 45 minutes. With the GS3s the train no longer needed piloting up the long 756-foot (230.4-m) climb of 16.5 miles (26.5 km) between San Luis Obispo and Santa Margarita. The locomotives were air-smoothed and finished in an orange, red and black color scheme which matched the special 'Daylight' rolling stock. At peak traffic periods the train consisted of 14 cars weighing 650 US tons/580 UK tons/590 tonnes. It was not a route for high speeds, the maximum rarely exceeding 80 mph (129 kph).

In 1938 the Association of American Railroads carried out tests with existing locomotive classes to establish principles for future design which it was hoped would enable a train of 1000 US tons/893 UK tons/907 tonnes to be accelerated to 100 mph (161 kph) and held at that speed on level track. The types tested were a Chicago & North Western 4—6—4, a pair of Pennsylvania K4 Pacifics and a Union Pacific 4—8—4. The UP engine came closest to target, accelerating 1005 US tons/897 UK tons/912 tonnes to 89 mph (143 kph) up 1-in-660 and touching 102.4 mph (164.8 kph) on a 1-in-500 downgrade. An

improved version of the UP 4—6—4 followed, designed specifically for 100 mph (161 kph) running and a top speed of 110 mph (177 kph). Driving-wheel diameter was increased from 6 feet 5 inches (1956 mm) to 6 feet 8 inches (2032 mm). Engines of this new series ran without change over the 1026 miles (1651.1 km) between Omaha and Salt Lake City, and the 1394 miles (2243.4 km) between Omaha and Huntington, Oregon.

By this time large American locomotives were being fitted with roller bearings throughout, a working application of the low rolling resistance qualities which had been demonstrated in an unusual manner by the Timken company in 1930. Timken had a 4—8—4 locomotive specially built by Alco as a demonstration unit, with tapered rolling bearings in all axleboxes and motion points. A photograph of the period shows it being pulled along by three men heaving on a rope (although it has been suggested that there may have been hidden manpower at the rear to get it on the move). This locomotive made lengthy demonstration tours and was eventually bought by the Northern Pacific Railroad, which used it for years in ordinary traffic.

The Norfolk & Western introduced its streamlined J class 4—8—4 in 1941. One of the class is claimed to have achieved 110 mph (177 kph) on the level during a special test on the Pennsylvania Railroad near Crestline, although the coupled wheels were of relatively small diameter – 5 feet 9 inches (1753 mm). In daily running on their own system the Js handled trains of 14 or 15 cars over gradients between 1-in-100 and 1-in-200 and regularly achieved 90 mph (145 kph).

The Canadian National Railways were consistent users of 4—8—4s over a long period, beginning in 1927, and finally had a fleet of 150, not counting those built for its Grand Trunk Western subsidiary. Many of them lasted to the end of steam in 1960. Construction of the 4—8—4s continued until 1942. Although they formed ten different classes, certain features were common throughout. Only the air-smoothed engines built in 1936 and a batch for the Grand Trunk Western of the same year interrupted the basic 25.5 by 30-inch (648 by 762-mm) cylinders and 6-foot 1-inch (1854-mm) diameter coupled wheels. The two batches of 1936, ten locomotives in all, had cylinders measuring 24 by 30 inches (610 by 762 mm) and 6-foot 5-inch (1956-mm) diameter coupled wheels.

The Canadian National was not the first of Canada's great railways and indeed was not planned as a nationwide system. Those distinctions fell to the Canadian Pacific Railway, which was incorporated in February 1881 after extensive survey work by parties of explorers who ventured into wild country to seek out a transcontinental route. By the end of the century the CPR had taken over many small railway companies which had existed in the provinces of Quebec and Ontario since the 1850s.

The task of building the line was a daunting one for the route traversed rocky outcrops, swamps, mountain passes, ravines, cliff edges, hundreds of miles of prairie and the great chain of the Rocky Mountains. Nevertheless, the new company, supported by the government, pushed the line east and west from Winnipeg so rapidly that in four years the line from Vancouver in British Columbia to Montreal on the St Lawrence River was completed, in spite of the fact that William Van Horne, the general manager,

**Below:** A Union Pacific 4—8—4 heads a northbound evening passenger train at Denver, Colorado.

**Right:** New York Central Railroad Westbound freight at Dunkirk, New York, behind 4—8—2 No 3113.
**Below right:** Southern Pacific Railroad 4—8—4 No 4436 at San Francisco, California.

Below: A Union Pacific 'Challenger' class 4–6–6–4 Mallet storms through the Weber Canyon with a heavy freight.

Above: Union Pacific 4–12–2 No 9044 leads 47 cars at an estimated 30 mph near Sherman in 1947.

Above left: An eastbound extra freight of 64 cars is headed near Sherman, Wyoming, by 4–6–6–4 No 3993.

Left: UP 4–6–6–4 No 3967 has a spell of passenger work as it pulls out of Denver for Cheyenne with the Denver Post Frontier Days Special, a promotional exercise by the local Denver Newspaper taking guests free of charge and with meals and refreshments 'on the house' to an annual rodeo.

Above: A red Canadian Pacific Railway Pacific No 2471 with an evening commuter train leaving Windsor station, Montreal. Right: Canadian Pacific 4–6–2 No 2413 takes an eastbound passenger train out of Toronto.

Above: A Canadian
National Railway 4–6–4
No 5700 at Toronto depot.

described one section — the north-shore stretch — as 200 miles of engineering impossibilities.

James Coughlin, a roadmaster on that section, later described conditions:

'We had to ride six or seven miles from the boarding cars to the track-laying machine on open flatcars when the thermometer registered 40 to 50° F below zero (40 to 46° C below zero). We would stand together in close groups and when the front men could not stand it any longer they would go round to the opposite side of the gang, and thus we kept moving until we reached work. . . . We had to use a tin stove and a piece of heavy zinc to heat the spikes sufficiently to prevent frozen heads from snapping off when they were being driven into the ties. We often found that the ties would split from end to end, so intense was the cold, if the spike turned on striking the sap.'

The first regular passenger train did not run from the east into Vancouver until 23 May 1887 (the intervening period was used to improve the track). In succeeding years as the company became more profitable, many of the original 'temporary' structures such as the dramatic timber-trestle viaducts, built from wood from nearby forests, were replaced with permanent steel constructions.

Canadian National was officially created in 1923 though the name had been used since 1919. Its formation took place in stages which involved the acquisition of several small railways and the Canadian Northern Railway (CNoR), the publicly owned Canadian Government Railway (CGR) and the British-owned Grand Trunk Railway (GTR), which was the oldest of these three and included the country's first railway, the Champlain & St Lawrence, built to a 5-foot 6-inch (1.67-m) gauge and opened on 21 July 1836.

Left: A formidable sight confronts any motorist or pedestrian venturing over this rudimentary crossing as Union Pacific 4–6–6–4 No 3999 bears down with an express freight.
Right: One of Union Pacific's 'Big Boy' 4–8–8–4s blasts through a cutting near Hermosa Tunnel, Wyoming, with a train of mixed freight.

Left: A pair of 2–8–8–2s of the Denver & Rio Grande Western lend their muscle at the rear of a freight train climbing a bank.
Below left: One of the Southern Pacific's 4–8–8–2s built in 1937 with the boiler 'turned round' so that the cab is at the front, heads 61 cars near Lang, California. The 'cab-at-front' layout improved conditions for the crew in tunnels.

The Canadian Pacific used 4–8–4s to a smaller extent than the CNR but began early with two locomotives built in its own works in 1928. Both companies used 4–6–4s during their period of intense competition in 1932 between Montreal and Toronto, when for a time they displaced the 'Cheltenham Flyer' from its place as 'the fastest train in the world.' The CPR 4–6–4s on this service were built in 1929 and were characterized by huge boilers and fireboxes designed for continuous heavy steaming. The 'Cheltenham Flyer' soon reasserted itself, but in fairness to the Canadians it should be mentioned that they were working much heavier trains – 672 US tons/600 UK tons/610 tonnes compared with the Flyer's usual 280 US tons/250 UK tons/254 tonnes.

Canadian Pacific steam is best remembered for its mountain-climbing ability on the transcontinental route. From Calgary the line climbs into the mountains for 120 miles (193 km) to reach the Kicking Horse Pass. The stiffest gradients are in the last four miles (6.4 km) to the summit where they steepen to 1-in-40 on sharp curves. Here the line crosses the Continental Divide between Alberta and British Columbia and then descends for 13 miles (21 km) to Field with an average gradient of 1-in-52. This was the home of the 5800 series of 2–10–2s employed on banking trains over the 'hill,' and they were sometimes joined on these duties by the celebrated 2–10–4s of the 'Selkirk' class, although both also worked the head. A pair of 'Selkirks' or a 2–10–2 and a 'Selkirk' hauling a heavy passenger train through the mountain section was a sight expressive of steam power in its ultimate development. Lighter trains were worked by the G4a class passenger Pacifics, and freight was generally in charge of 2–8–2s assisted by a 2–10–2 or 2–10–4.

A train such as the eastbound 'Dominion' would be divided to run through the mountain section in two parts, separated by an interval of about ten minutes,

and each part might be heavy enough to be double-headed. Up they would go with the engines in full gear and full regulator, shooting their exhaust 100 feet high up into the sky. The mountains would reverberate with the noise and then suddenly, mysteriously, fall silent, for just as the leading portion entered the upper of the two spiral tunnels on the section the second part would be entering the lower tunnel. After a brief pause the exhausts hammered out again as the trains wound their way to the summit, speed barely exceeding 10 mph (16 kph). Westbound trains crawled down the hill at about the same speed with great caution, the bells on the locomotives clanging continuously. At night the spectacle had a new fascination. Watchers on the mountain slopes could follow the progress of a train as a string of lights crawling along the rock face. They would disappear into the first spiral tunnel, then be glimpsed again higher up and moving in the opposite direction as the train emerged. Another blackout followed as it was swallowed by the upper tunnel, then the lights were seen again, higher still and having changed direction a second time.

North America had its 12-coupled rigid-frame locomotives on the Union Pacific, built for working fast freight between Ogden, Idaho and Cheyenne, Wyoming, a distance of 483 miles (777.3 km). The first appeared in 1926 and four years later the railway had a fleet of 86. Ogden-Cheyenne is a mountain section with a long climb of 1-in-88 going east. After the summit there is easier going to Laramie with a ruling gradient of 1-in-125, but from there to Cheyenne most of the way is down a continuous gradient averaging 1-in-83 with two steep sections at 1-in-66. Westbound trains starting out of Cheyenne were faced with a climb of this severity extending for 31 miles (50 km). The UP had some Mallet articulated compounds in service, but their speed over the easier sections of the route was too low to maintain the necessary flow of traffic without

Above: East Broad Top Railroad 2—8—2 No 17 working for her living with a coal train before the line became part of the leisure industry.
Above left: The pull-out regulator and brake controller in a typical US steam locomotive cab layout. Note the engineer's gauntlets.
Left: Accelerating after picking up cars, a narrow-gauge Denver & Rio Grande Western freight train near Alamosa emits a sculptured plume of smoke.

impeding passenger trains. There were also some ten-coupled engines but axle-load limitations ruled out development of a more powerful design with this wheel arrangement. The railway therefore felt obliged to go to a 12-coupled design, and with the heavy piston thrust that would be necessary it had to be a three-cylinder engine with divided drive.

The UP 4—12—2s were the largest three-cylinder engines ever built. The coupled wheelbase was 30 feet 8 inches (9.35 m), which was 4 feet 5 inches (1.35 m) longer than that of the closest equivalent in this respect, the Bulgarian 2—12—4T. To get the engine safely around curves the leading single-axle truck had a controlled lateral movement of 6.25 inches (158 mm), while the first and sixth coupled axles were allowed a spring-cushioned sideplay of 1 inch (25.4 mm). The thickness and spacing of the driving wheel flanges varied; originally the fourth pair of driving wheels were flangeless but had wider treads than the others. Thin flanges were added later. The two outside cylinders measured 27 by 32 inches (686 by 813 mm) and the inside cylinder 27 by 31 inches (686 by 787 mm). Boiler pressure was 220 lb per square inch (15.5 kg/sq cm). As built the class had two sets of Walschaerts valve gear. The valve of the inside cylinder was originally driven by rocking levers on the Gresley principle, but this arrangment was removed and a third set of Walschaerts gear was fitted later.

In service the locomotives increased the traffic capacity of the section between Green River and Laramie by 44 percent compared with what the 2—10—0s could shift. They could take 4000 US tons/ 3571 UK tons/3628 tonnes from Ogden up the bank to Green River, cruising on level stretches at 35 to 40 mph (56 to 64 kph). Banking assistance was pro-

vided uphill when loads reached 125 cars. Coming west from Cheyenne trains were banked up the 31 miles (49.8 km) of continuous gradient whatever the head-end power. The 4—12—2s could take the same load as a Mallet on this section at a slightly higher speed. In the late 1930s, however, they were joined by a new family of UP articulated locomotives – the 4—6—6—4s of the 'Challenger' class – and some were transferred to the Idaho Division of the system.

As conceived by its inventor, Anatole Mallet, the locomotive named after him was a compound, but its distinctive feature was its articulated construction. Purists sometimes object that an articulated locomotive on Mallet's system but with simple propulsion is not a Mallet, but the objection is over-ruled by common usage. A locomotive built on the Mallet system actually comprises two steam engines, the rear one in a fixed frame and the leading one in a separate truck which can swing about a pivot at the rear and is coupled to the rear engine by an articulated joint through which the tractive effort is transmitted. The forward end of the boiler and smokebox is supported by a bearing surface on the leading truck. Basically this was the arrangement of the 'Challenger' class, plus leading and trailing guiding bogies, but the front and rear engines were three-cylinder simple-expansion machines, and developments in articulation and bearers had produced a Mallet-style locomotive suitable for speeds around 60 mph (97 kph), which was what the Union Pacific needed for its fastest freight services. Alco supplied UP with 105 of these locomotives. Others by the same builder went to Delaware & Hudson, Denver & Rio Grande Western, Western Pacific and the Clinchfield Rail-road of Tennessee. The United States was an in-veterate user of Mallets, both compound and simple-expansion, dating back to some Alco 0—6—6—0 units on the Baltimore & Ohio in 1903.

The 'Challengers' pointed ahead to the ultimate in the American Mallet, again produced for the Ogden–Green River section of the Union Pacific. These were the 4000 class 4—8—8—4s of 1942—44, better known as the 'Big Boys.' The nearest previous approaches to an articulated locomotive of comparable size had been the Northern Pacific 2—8—8—4 of 1927 and the Southern Pacific 4—8—8—2 of 1937, the latter built 'back-to-front' so that the cab and the four-wheel bogie were at the leading end, and the crew was less troubled by the exhaust in long single-line tunnels.

The 'Big Boys' were special-purpose machines, destined not only for a particular route but also for a particular traffic – fast fruit trains of 70 refrigerator cars. They were therefore designed for a top speed of 70 mph (113 kph). Appearing in 1941, however, they were soon plunged into wartime traffic conditions which made the 3200 US tons/2857 UK tons/ 2902 tonnes of the fruit trains seem relatively modest and soon loads were being hauled over the gradients at both ends of the Ogden–Cheyenne line that needed two 'Big Boys' in tandem. These were the largest and heaviest steam locomotives ever built, weighing 534 US tons/477 UK tons/484 tonnes with engine and tender and measuring 132 feet 11 inches (40.5 m) overall. The tender ran on 14 wheels, consisting of a leading four-wheel truck and a ten-wheel fixed wheel-base, and carried 25 US tons/22 UK tons/23 tonnes of coal and 25,000 US gallons/20,817 UK gallons/ 94,635 liters of water. Majestic in every respect, the 'Big Boys' were a worthy finale to the international cavalcade of Mallet articulated locomotives.

# 4. Standardization in Germany

Political events did much to shape the development of the steam locomotive in Germany. When the German Empire was founded in 1871, the various state systems found themselves working alongside a host of private companies which were supplied with locomotives by a highly competitive industry whose member firms were more interested in stamping their products with their own individuality than in moving toward any measure of uniformity. The Prussian State Railways were the first to tackle the problem of deciding which classes to retain and what should be built in the future.

Although the lack of standardization had been severely felt in military transport during the war of 1870, most of the state systems failed to learn the lesson and continued building locomotives in rich variety. In Prussia, however, two standard types were introduced as early as 1877 – a 2–4–0 for passenger traffic and a 2–6–0 for freight traffic – and in the next five years 11 more designs were approved for construction. Nonetheless Germany entered the 1914–1918 war with a locomotive stock almost as variegated as before, although this time the consequences were more serious. A demand for standardization in 1917 came too late.

Political changes after 1918 brought amalgamation of the state systems into the Deutsche Reichsbahn in 1920. The new organization took over more than 350 different types of steam locomotive but as a result of wartime losses, reparations and serious arrears of repairs the stock of serviceable motive power was much depleted. Quick action was necessary. First the well-proven types of the former individual state railways were reviewed and it was proposed to select a limited number for further building using standard components. This idea was later discarded, however, and it was decided to build a completely new range of standard types. For this purpose the newly formed Transport Ministry set up a committee of specialists from the railways and the locomotive manufacturing industry to lay down essential guidelines for developing a new fleet of steam locomotives, and to decide on the types to be built.

Eventually the committee created a Standardization Office to which was entrusted the task not simply of agreeing on principles but of producing complete designs for the new locomotives, working in collaboration with the manufacturers who would produce them. By 1922 the Office had approved 14 designs, including two Pacifics with 6-foot 3-inch (1905 mm) wheels for express passenger traffic, one of which (class 01) was a two-cylinder simple, and the other (class 02) a four-cylinder compound. Although opinion generally favored simple propulsion it was

Left: Ex-Prussian P8 class 4–6–0s continued to be built after grouping of the individual State Railways into the Reichsbahn. No 038 772–0 leaves Wolfrach, now in Western Germany, with a local train. Right: Another view of 038 772–0 at Wolfrach.

decided to make a practical comparison between the two systems before completing the program. No overall advantage was found in compounding, however, and the 02s were converted to class 01 simple Pacifics between 1938 and 1942.

The first of the standard locomotives to appear was 02 compound Pacific No 02.001 which Henschel completed in time for it to be shown at the German Transport Exhibition in Munich in September 1925. Later in the same year the first 01 class locomotives were ready, while 1926 saw the two 2–10–0 goods (or freight) locomotive classes, 43 and 44. In all, locomotives of 29 standard classes were built between 1925 and 1945, both tender and tank engines to cover all types of duty – the range was extended to cover changing circumstances first in peacetime conditions and then in war.

In the early years of the plan deliveries of certain

classes of locomotives which had been operated by the former individual state railways continued while others were modified to improve their performance. Among the latter was the ex-Prussian State Railways P8 class 4–6–0 which, although dating from 1906 and of obsolescent design, remained a versatile and economical locomotive and a favorite with the staff. One reason for keeping the older designs in service was that the two Pacific classes were built with an axle-load of 22 US tons/20 UK tons/20 tonnes, which was too heavy for some of the main lines, and some time elapsed before all important routes could be brought up to the 20-ton standard. Soon, however, a new light Pacific with the same wheel diameter as the 01s but 20 US-ton/18 UK-ton/18-tonne axle-load was added to the standard classes. A preproduction series of three locomotives was turned out by Borsig in 1930. Full production began in the following year and continued until 1938. These engines were class 03. The class 44 2–10–0 was a three-cylinder simple, and as the transport requirements of the expanding Reich grew, other three-cylinder classes were introduced: the 05 streamlined 4–6–4, the 06 4–8–4, the class 45 2–10–2 and the heavy freight 2–10–2 tank locomotives of classes 84 and 85. There were also variations of earlier two-cylinder designs in three-cylinder form, such as the 01¹⁰ streamlined Pacific class on which construction began in 1939. Orders had been placed for 250 of these locomotives but only 55 were completed when building was halted in 1940 to allow manufacturers to concentrate on wartime 'austerity' 2–10–0s.

Certain features ran through all the standard classes. Working pressure in the principal types rose from previous levels to 227 lb per square inch (16 kg/sq cm). Simple expansion with long-travel piston valves was general after the rejection of compounding. All locomotives had bar frames. In classes with a wide firebox, the trailing truck was set well back from the rear coupled axle to obtain optimum air inlet and ash removal conditions. A row of fitments lent interest to the top of the boiler, including a pump-operated feedwater heater, two domes (one covering the top feed arrangement from the feedwater heater) and one or, on ten-coupled engines, two large-capacity sandboxes. There were no splashers and the driving wheels revolved fully exposed beneath high running plates. Smoke deflector plates extended downward to the running plate but after the war these were replaced by a shallower version supported from the smokebox with its lower edge well above running-plate level. All engines had to pass through a loading gauge 13 feet 9.5 inches (4.2 m) high, which meant a very low chimney on large-boilered locomotives. However, detachable extensions were provided and these were virtually a permanent fixture on locomotives allocated to the principal main lines where a height of 14 feet 11 inches (4.5 m) was permitted. Commentators have noted how closely the general appearance of the standard locomotives approximated to that of the Prussian State Railway designs.

New locomotives were tested on the road with a special test train consisting of a dynamometer car and brake locomotives which was based at Grünewald. At that time the General Manager of the Reichsbahn was Dr Julius Dorpmüller, an engineer by training, who would often appear unannounced at Grünewald to accompany the train when important tests were afoot. These were pleasant occasions, much appreciated by the staff, concluding with a repast of smoked ham and the best champagne thoughtfully provided by the general manager himself. Grünewald was equipped with a roller test plant for express locomotives on which two-cylinder types could 'run' at 50 mph (81 kph) and three- or four-cylinder types at 62 mph (100 kph). A Prussian P8 was once pushed up to 74 mph (119 kph). However, it was difficult to keep slidebars and crossheads cool without the normal draft caused by motion and the slidebars of the P8 became red hot after 20 minutes. The 03 Pacifics could not be tested on the plant.

'Design by committee' seems unlikely to bring individual personalities to the fore, but the guiding spirit of Reichsbahn design, Dr R P Wagner, was well known throughout the locomotive world. He had been associated with the work from its inception and from his appointment as Chief of Motive Power Construction for the Reichsbahn in July 1923 he presided over its progress for two decades. Wagner's writings, and his technical papers delivered to institutions and learned societies both within and outside Germany earned him international recognition; it was his particular pride to have been elected an Honorary Member of the British Institution of Locomotive Engineers and to be the only German Member of the Royal Society. A British railway engineer who met him in the 1930s remembered him as 'a great bear of a man' and noted that his observance of the salutes and greetings which had become mandatory among German officialdom was somewhat perfunctory compared with that of certain of his colleagues. This independence of mind and behavior had its effect on his career in the war years. In contemporary pictures Wagner is unmistakable, usually being the tallest member of any group.

Experiment proceeded in parallel with standardization. In 1928 a Pacific was built with a Löffler high-pressure boiler in which steam was generated at 120 atmospheres in a special drum and fed to the high-pressure cylinders. The exhaust, at 18 atmospheres, passed through a heat-exchanger and the condensate was returned to the drum. The central low-pressure cylinder took steam from the boiler at 15 atmospheres, which was exhausted into the atmosphere and provided the draft for the fire. A very high degree of superheat was used.

The trials, mostly between Potsdam, Burg and Magdeburg, were not without incident. A colleague of Wagner's recalls an occasion when one of the tubes in the high-pressure section of the firebox burst. Steam escaped into the inner firebox with a deafening noise, forcing red-hot coals through the grate into the ashpan. Luckily the firedoor was closed, but it was distorted by the pressure and the cab was filled with a cloud of coal dust. The crew and observers on the footplate emerged from the incident unharmed but as black as chimney sweeps. A representative of the builders, Schwartzkopff, accompanied the locomotive on its trials, and the same source recalls that despite this and other less dramatic mishaps his confidence was never shaken. Some of the Reichsbahn officers were less sure. It was so often necessary to take the locomotive off the train at Kirchmoser, where there was a repair facility, that the place became known as 'Schwartzkopff's Rest.' The locomotive was never taken over by the Reichsbahn. After lying idle for a few years at the builder's works it was finally cut up. A clause in the contract required Schwartzkopff to replace the high-pressure locomotive with a standard class 01 Pacific should the former prove unsuitable

for service but, in the end, a class 03 Pacific was supplied to settle the affair.

Krupp and Maffei each built a 4–6–2 turbine locomotive for the Reichsbahn in the 1920s and both were taken into the railway's stock with the numbers T 18 1001 and T 18 1002 respectively. The Krupp locomotive was damaged by bombing and taken out of service in 1940 but during its working life had yielded very favorable fuel consumption results. The Maffei locomotive was less successful in this respect. It was withdrawn and broken up in the war years.

The 1930s saw the zenith of the steam locomotive in Germany, spurred on by the demand for faster trains between the principal cities in the country and the revised Reichsbahn timetable of 1924. Competition from electric and diesel motive power was also beginning to be felt, particularly in the proliferation of fast railcar services. Early in the decade Borsig had experimented with streamlining Pacifics Nos

03.154 and 03.193 (lighter versions of the 01 class). Although the results did not fulfill expectations, the tests led to the building of the fully streamlined class 05 4–6–4s, designed specifically for working non-stop supplementary-fare trains between Berlin and Hamburg. They were required to run continuously on the level with a 280-US-ton/250-UK-ton/254-tonne train at 93 mph (150 kph) – the normal maximum for steam locomotives – but to be capable of 109 mph (175 kph) if necessary to regain time. They departed from the standard classes in various respects, for example the 7-foot 6.5-inch (2300-mm) driving wheels and the 284 lb per square inch (20 kg/sq cm) boiler pressure. Nos 05.001 and 05.002 appeared in the German railway centenary year, 1935, and earned Wagner a Gold Medal from the British Institution of Locomotive Engineers, an honor which had not been conferred for some time previously. A third member of the class produced in 1938 was equipped to burn pulverized coal and had the cab at the front.

Above: East Germany left some of the 01s in their original condition, among them 01036, seen leaving Bebra, the border station, with a Frankfurt–Cottbus train on 20 May 1967.

**Above right:** The three-cylinder 01¹⁰ Pacifics of 1937 were later renumbered 011 (coal-fired) and 012 (oil-fired). No 012 001–4 waits at Westerland on the Island of Sylt with a train for Hamburg.

In 1936 No 05.002 achieved a world-record speed for steam of 124.5 mph (200.4 kph) with a special 336-US-ton/300-UK-ton/305-tonne test train. It was a triumph for the design team, heightened by the current rivalry with the high-speed diesel railcars. A humorous drawing showed No 05.002, which had an exterior somewhat like a whale, opening its stream-lined smokebox casing like a pair of jaws to swallow what was apparently the 'Flying Hamburger.' Wagner had a print of the drawing on the wall of his office behind his desk. When the British Institution of Loco-motive Engineers held its summer meeting in Germany in 1936, No 05.002 worked a special train for the delegates from Berlin to Hamburg and back. The load, with four coaches and a dynamometer car, was 158 US ton/141 UK tons/143 tonnes. After stopping at Wittenberge the train ran the next 27.4 miles (44 km) to Ludwigslust in 20 minutes 58 seconds, averaging 111.6 mph (179.6 kph) for 4.7 miles (7.5 km) and reaching a maximum of 118 mph (190 kph).

On the return trip a broken water connection between engine and tender necessitated an emergency stop which was made good from a speed of nearly 100 mph (161 kph) in exactly 60 seconds. After temporary repairs at Wittenberge the 70.1 miles (112.8 km) to a signal stop 13.9 miles (22.4 km) outside Berlin were run at an average speed of 86.7 mph (139.5 kph) with a top speed of 103.5 mph (166.6 kph). Steam trains on the Berlin–Hamburg route at this period were normally restricted to a maximum of 93 mph (150 kph) but were required to average 74.2 mph (119.4 kph) from Berlin to Hamburg and 73.7 mph (118.6 kph) in the reverse direction. The 03 Pacifics of the standard series, but streamlined, performed equally well on this route.

Wagner's reaction to the *Mallard* speed record of 1938 seems to have lacked enthusiasm. In a speech on one occasion he could not resist commenting that it had been achieved down a gradient of 1-in-200 (the 05.002 record had been on the level) and he quoted a comment attributed to Charles S Lake, technical editor of the British journal *The Railway Gazette*, that there might justifiably be doubts as to whether the Blue Ribbon of speed for steam had in fact been wrested from Germany.

Compounding reappeared briefly in 1932 in con-nection with experiments with a 'medium-pressure' boiler working at 25 atmospheres ('medium' in rela-tion to the 120 atmospheres high-pressure boiler in the Schwartzkopff experiment). The 25 atmospheres pressure was considered too high for expansion in a single stage and so orders were placed for two com-pound Pacifics and a compound 2–10–0 freight locomotive; also for a 4–6–0 on the Stumpf/Wagner system. Professor Stumpf had devised a system based on stationary engine practice at the beginning of the century in which expanded steam was exhausted half-way through the piston stroke through a ring of orifices at the middle of the cylinder. The main ports therefore only passed live steam at high temperature and condensation on the cylinder walls was reduced. The experiments were short-lived but the Pacifics were rebuilt with a normal-pressure boiler and re-numbered 02.101/2. In this form they worked alongside other 02s on the Leipzig-Hof-Regensburg section of the important north-south express route from Berlin to Munich. The Berlin–Leipzig section was the province of 01s and 03s as well as former Prussian P10s and S10¹s.

Although the streamlining of the two 03s by Borsig was not followed up at once, more of these engines (built in 1939) were streamlined and classi-fied 03¹⁰. A contemporary of the 05 class streamlined 4–6–4s was a high-speed streamlined tank engine of the same wheel arrangement, No 61.001, which, after trials and demonstration runs, went into service between Berlin and Dresden with a train of special coaches designed by the Wegmann Company. A similar tank engine, but with an additional axle in the trailing truck, giving it the unusual 4–6–6 wheel arrangement, followed in 1939.

Wagner's career reached its climax in the middle

1930s. In the second half of the decade there were signs that his star was setting. His powers were diminished by a new organization at Reichsbahn headquarters, and his future was not helped by his attitude to the Nazi Party. He once described the Rome–Berlin axis as 'a cheap tin tube for blowing hot air across the Alps' and he was less than complimentary about the eagle symbols in aluminum with which the Reichsbahn proposed to adorn its locomotives. In this tense atmosphere criticism of some

mountain retreat, a young engineer approached the Doctor and asked to take his photograph standing in front of the engine. Wagner shook his head. 'No,' he said, 'the return crank arm's too short.' He already showed signs of nervous strain, and when a crash program of locomotive building for the war effort was launched under the direction of Albert Speer, Minister for Armaments and Munitions, it was clear that the future lay with younger men. Wagner retired on health grounds on 1 October 1942.

Above: A postwar Reichsbahn light Pacific of the prewar Reichsbahn's 03 class is studied with interest by an observer in Leipzig Hbf.

aspects of his standard locomotive policy flourished, and centered particularly on the development of a large streamlined three-cylinder 4–8–4 for duties which were beyond the capacity of the 03 Pacifics. A feature of the design was that by adjustment of the weight on the bogies, the driving axle-load could be set at either 20 or 22 US tons/18 or 20 UK tons/18 or 20 tonnes. This was class 06 of 1939. Only two engines were built. The international crisis and the outbreak of war imposed a complete revision of locomotive building policy in which Wagner played a diminishing part.

Seeing his precepts set aside while he was still in office was a bitter experience for Wagner. There is a memory of him at Berchtesgarden in 1942 during trials of a new 2–6–2 for secondary passenger service for which he was responsible. During a stop in the newly built Berchtesgarden station with its platforms for receiving special trains conveying Party leaders, Ministers and deputations to visit the Führer in his

After the war Wagner's reputation outside Germany as a locomotive engineer earned him an appointment through the British occupation authorities to the Reichsbahn management in Bielfeld where he headed a group concerned with the ordering and distribution of materials and acted as a liaison officer between the railroads and the Allies until a second retirement. Thereafter he continued to serve as an Honorary Member of the Locomotive Committee of the Bundesbahn, interesting himself particularly in questions of metallurgy and filing patents on this subject when in his seventies. In 1952, to his great pleasure, his membership of the Institution of Locomotive Engineers and of the Royal Society, suspended during the war, was restored. He died after a short illness on 14 February 1953.

Up to the war the German locomotive building firms pursued their individual development programs and, indeed, once orders for standard locomotives had been placed, by the later 1930s they were intro-

Above: The class 65 2–8–4 tanks were a Bundesbahn design, appearing in 1951, but were soon displaced by diesels. No 065 001–0 sails through leafy setting at Laudenbach.

ducing detail features of their own as construction proceeded. One product of this period was overtaken by the war – a Henschel locomotive with its four driving axles individually powered by two-cylinder vee-form steam engines which was not completed until 1941. The birth of the idea, however can be traced back to 1937 when two Henschel engineers had discussions with the Reichsbahn on the steam railcars they were developing, with the emphasis on burning cheaper fuel. This project was running into problems and seemed liable to be cancelled. Henschel had to find something new to interest the steam partisans in the Reichsbahn, who already saw themselves challenged in some areas by the success of the high-speed diesel railcars. A small two-cylinder steam engine had been developed as a blower and feed pump drive for one of the Henschel steam rail-cars and it was decided that this could be developed for traction. The outcome was the construction of the Reichsbahn's 1–Do–1 locomotive No 19.001. In

appearance the high-speed steam engines, with their two cylinders forming a 90-degree vee, were similar to an internal combustion engine. They were mounted alternately on the right-hand and left-hand sides of the main frames and drove the axles directly through flexible couplings. Although designed for a top speed of 110 mph (177 kph) the driving wheels were only of 4 feet 1.25 inches (1251 mm) in diameter which gave locomotives a very high maximum tractive effort. The valve gear and piston valves were enclosed in an oil-tight casing forming a unit with the crankcase. The locomotive was fully streamlined although the casing was slightly raised along the driving wheelbase.

From the first trials it was evident that there would be no question of early introduction of the locomotive in regular express service. The boiler did not steam well, the drawgear lacked strength, and there was some leakage of steam past the piston rings. This may have contributed to an exceptionally high steam consumption which limited the radius of action of the

**Above: Class 23 No 23 047 threads the intricacies of the layout through the yards at Saarbrücken. Previous page: A postwar DB class 23 mixed traffic 2–6–2 leaves Bullay with the 17.00 to Trier on 28 August 1969.**

locomotive in spite of its high-capacity tender. Tractive effort did not remain constant for a particular setting of the controls but was found to increase although no alteration had been made. All these and other problems required investigation on a scale which was not practical in wartime. No 19.001 went into retreat near Hamburg until the end of the war, when it was sent to the United States for further study of its possibilities. However, steam-locomotive building in the United States was already in decline and in 1952 the locomotive was scrapped.

The war brought a four-year plan of locomotive construction, reorganization of the locomotive industry on mass-production lines, and an end to individual initiative by the locomotive building firms. Construction continued of the 2–10–0 standard freight 50 class locomotive which had been introduced in 1938. The design was soon simplified in some respects and the later engines reclassified 50UK (*Ubergangs-kriegslokomotiv*). As more territories became occupied in Europe the demand for motive power grew continuously, and after control of production was taken over by the Ministry of Armaments and Munitions in 1942 a new design of 2–10–0 was introduced. It was generally similar to the 50 class but planned to economize in man-hours for construction and in scarce materials. It was called

class 52. Over 6000 were built, many of them coming from works outside Germany.

The war in Russia took German locomotives deep into a territory with meager provision for watering. Further class 52s were therefore built with condensing tenders and classified 52KON. Their equipment differed from that of the rest of the class, for as the exhaust steam was led back to the condensing tender the draft had to be supplied by a fan in the smokebox driven by an exhaust turbine. Further exhaust turbines drove the fans in the tender that drew air through the cooling elements. The flow was regulated by adjustable shutters which could be closed altogether in severe weather. With this equipment the locomotives could run 625 miles (1005.8 km) without rewatering, an ability which proved valuable during the withdrawal from Russia when water supplies were destroyed by Soviet troops or partisans, as well as during the initial advance.

All these classes had axle-loads between 17 and 18 US tons/15 and 16 UK tons/15 and 16 tonnes. A heavier locomotive was proposed in 1942 and materialized a year later as the class 42 2–10–0. Maximum axle-load for most of the class was 20 US tons/18 tons/18 tonnes but a series for the Austrian railways was modified in various ways to reduce this figure to 19 US tons/17 UK tons/17 tonnes.

Cylinder bore in class 42 was increased by 1.18 inches (29.9 mm) to take advantage of the higher adhesive weight. Classes 50, 52 and 42 were known collectively as the *Kriegslokomotiven* War locomotives); over 8000 were built between 1941 and 1945 and many of them found widespread use in the postwar years.

The long survival of main-line steam in Western and Eastern Germany after the war may seem surprising considering the development of long-distance electric traction in the country. As the European crisis deepened in the late 1930s, however, strategic considerations imposed too great a commitment for any motive power with its range of action limited by an electrical supply system which, moreover, was vulnerable to attack. In the immediate aftermath of the war locomotive building in Germany was not permitted but the ban was lifted in 1950. After the division of the country, West Germany had about 17,700 steam locomotives, a total which far exceeded its requirements. A wave of scrapping began, in which survivors of the pre-Reichsbahn State systems suffered most. Seven new classes were proposed embodying developments in construction and practice which had taken place since the '1925 Standard,' but in the end only five were built, and in limited quantities. At the same time existing classes

which were suitable for retention were modernized. New boilers with combustion chambers were designed for the Pacific Classes 01, 03, and their three-cylinder variants, $01^{10}$ and $03^{10}$. The three-cylinder 01s had been put into store toward the end of the war but were returned to traffic after 1945 with their steamlining removed. Troubles developed in the all-welded boilers, however, and they went back into store until the middle 1950s. In its final years this series was reclassified 011 or, if fitted for oil-burning, 012.

The first postwar locomotives were class 82, a 0–10–0 design for the West German Bundesbahn Class 94 of the former Prussian State Railways. The first of 41 engines in this series appeared in 1950. Class 82 was employed on heavy shunting and slow passenger duties but had mechanical weaknesses in the arrangement for allowing radial movement of the leading and trailing pairs of coupled axles which led to frequent renewal of components. The last of the class was scrapped in the spring of 1972 at which time 24 of the ex-Prussian class 94 veterans they were intended to replace were still in service.

Class 23 also appeared in 1950. This was a mixed traffic 2–6–2 similar to the wartime locomotives of the same class. Only two of the originals were built, however, and they both remained in East Germany

after the war. The Bundesbahn class 23s were virtually a new design and differed appreciably from the forerunners in appearance with the removal of the top feed dome and sandboxes from the top of the boiler, while a wide-diameter chimney encircled the exhaust outlets of the air and feedwater pumps as well as the main exhaust from the cylinders. There were some superheater troubles with these engines and some were rebuilt for saturated steam. Riding was poor — a British commentator has written of 'a fore and aft shuttling motion' which could be felt in the train — and the weight distribution between the axles was the cause of other problems. Nonetheless, this was a numerous class, comprising 105 locomotives, and for some years worked international expresses between the Dutch border and Cologne.

In 1951 the first 2—8—4 tank engines of class 65 appeared but the class was soon outdated by the V100 diesels. Its maximum speed in passenger traffic of only 53 mph (85 kph) did not compare favorably with the ex-Prussian class 78 4—6—4 tanks, and although a powerful machine its usefulness in freight traffic was limited by its fuel capacity. Its axle-load of 19 US tons/17 UK tons/17 tonnes also restricted its employment on secondary lines. Only 18 of the class were built. The most successful postwar Bundesbahn design was the three-cylinder class 10 Pacific of 1958, but only two were built. With their good riding qualities at speed and economy in fuel consumption they would have had a distinguished future had they not been overtaken by the rapid development of electric and diesel traction.

In all the postwar steam locomotive designs special attention was given to the comfort of the crew. Cabs had large skylights in the roof, improved ventilation and footwarmers for winter use. Instruments were grouped together and all controls arranged so as to be accessible while seated. At the same time many locomotives of the East German Reichsbahn were modernized in various ways: roller bearings were fitted, equipment for oil-firing installed and so on. In the last days of steam in Western Germany the best-known locomotives to foreign visitors were the 01 and 03 Pacifics and survivors of the *Kriegslokomotiven*.

Pockets of main-line steam lasted until the 1970s. One result of the partition of Germany was that the importance of the town of Hof in northeast Bavaria as a junction of several principal north-south routes was diminished. The proximity of the new frontier virtually deprived it of a direct outlet to the north and as a result the lines through Hof were not electrified. The service from Hof westward to Lichtenfels remained almost 100 percent steam-worked until the end. (Some of the steam locomotives ran to and from Bamberg on the electrified line.) Tank locomotives of classes 64 and 86 continued to work branch lines in the Hof—Nürnberg—Schwandorf triangle. On the Lichtenfels line there is a five-mile gradient at 1-in-40 (the Schiefe Ebene) between Neuenmarkt—Wirsberg and Marktschorgast and it was here that (until 1973) 01 Pacifics could be seen and heard in the manner that delights the steam enthusiast. The last main-line steam workings in Western Germany were in the north of the country on the line from Rheine to Emden where 0 42s, 0 43s, 0 44s and 0 50s worked heavy mineral trains right into 1977.

Steam motive power in East Germany, where the Reichsbahn name has survived, was inherited from the West and remained virtually unchanged for ten years. Thereafter some of the older types were rebuilt,

including 01 Pacifics, which in their revised form presented a considerably altered appearance. The Reichsbahn administration introduced its own 2—6—2 design, classified 023[10], to replace the Prussian P8. The prewar 4—6—6 tank, already noted as the one used on the Berlin—Dresden one-class trains before the war, was rebuilt in 1961 as a 4—6—2 tender locomotive. Here, too, electric and diesel power made rapid inroads but steam lingered on a number of narrow-gauge lines.

In West Germany a renumbering system suitable for data processing by computer was introduced in 1968—69. Class 01, for example, became 001, the additional 0 representing a steam locomotive, and a seventh figure was added as a check digit. A typical number of an 01 Pacific would, therefore, be 001.088—4. The first three digits show motive power and class, the next three are the individual locomotive number, and the digit after the hyphen is derived from the others for checking purposes.

Before leaving the German railway scene it is worth recalling that Germany's school of locomotive design not only took ideas from other countries but also contributed a great deal to the design of others and exported a considerable number of ideas as well as locomotives.

Possibly the greatest advance in design since the earliest days of George Stephenson himself was the high-degree superheater developed by Wilhelm Schmidt. It was, indeed, one of the few locomotive features to be adopted on a truly worldwide basis. Its purpose was to reduce heat loss in the cylinders by eliminating condensation during admission and expansion and re-evaporation at exhaust. The incoming steam from the regulator was divided into a number of small tube elements each leading into an enlarged flue tube in the boiler. The result in the original design of 1902 was a gain of 20 to 30 percent in steam consumption. Its success was such that by 1914 it had become an almost universal feature on locomotives in many countries.

The work of Wagner and Professor Nordmann to establish the ideal relationship between boiler and tube dimensions and the flow of hot gases to obtain maximum steaming capacity and efficiency also established a formula which was applied universally in locomotive design. Many of the engines designed for the Reichsbahn after 1918 were subsequently to be seen in other countries, either in their original form or adapted to a particular country's needs. In France the Est was so impressed by the German G12 class 2—10—0s, it had acquired in 1919 as reparation for World War I damage that it built 195 similar engines under license from 1926. At the same time, Belgium received some 1960 German locomotives of 43 different types and many of these were still in service when the Nazis overran that country again in 1940 — and indeed were still being used for a decade after World War II. Poland, Bulgaria, Yugoslavia and Turkey also received large numbers of German locomotives or built them themselves. For Bulgaria, German manufacturers improved on their designs to produce locomotives suited to that country's needs.

Thus, it was by way of intentional exports and foreign manufacture under license, and by enforced dispersal as reparation after two world wars that the typically Teutonic locomotives — by no means beautiful but well-proportioned and thoroughly designed — had their influence on the steam railroads of many countries.

# 5. The Steam Locomotive in France

There still exists in some corners of the world the mistaken belief that the French are insensible to the fascination of the steam locomotive. To realize its falseness one has only to look at railway scenes painted by the French Impressionists of the 19th century, or preserved in words of such great novels as Emile Zola's *La Bête Humaine*.

To a generation that remembers the late 1930s, *La Bête Humaine* was a superb railway film, its action set in that period. Jean Renoir's film updated the novel, which ends in 1870 with a driverless troop train bound for the front in the Franco—Prussian war careering to inevitable destruction, filled with inebriated soldiers singing and shouting, unconscious of their doom. It is a curious book, its central character an engine driver who sees his locomotive as a living creature. On an early page there is a descriptive passage vibrant with the atmosphere of the steam railway, seen through the eyes of Rouband at Le Havre station:

'A powerful express engine with a single pair of huge driving wheels for eating up the miles, stood alone with smoke billowing from its chimney and climbing slowly straight upwards in the still air. But his attention was focused on the 3.25 to Caen, already loaded and waiting for its engine. He could not see the engine, for it was on the other side of the bridge, but he could hear it whistling impatiently for the road in a series of short, sharp blasts. An order was shouted, and acknowledged by an answering screech from the whistle. Then, before the engine moved off, there was a moment of silence, suddenly broken by the opening of the cylinder drain cocks and the deafening hiss of escaping steam sweeping along the tracks. He saw a great white cloud emerging from under the bridge, swirling and eddying like snow and climbing up through the girders. Half the scene before him was blotted out with white, while the thickening smoke from the other engine spread an ever-growing veil of black. Beyond the obscurity, the sound of shunters' horns, men's shouts and the clatter of turntables were half muffled. Part of the cloud thinned and was rent, and through the gap he saw two trains passing each other, one from Versailles which was running into the station and one on its way out to Auteuil.'

Such was the scene from the Pont de l'Europe, outside the Gare St Lazare, where now the electric trains pass with a sigh and a swish of the pantograph on the contact wire that are scarcely heard above the roar of the road traffic. There is a similar scene in a painting by Monet. One wonders which came first — whether Zola's words inspired Monet's brush or were a verbal interpretation of the canvas. The two men belonged to the same circle. They can be seen together in a group portrait in the Galérie du Jeu de Paume in Paris surrounded by other literary and artistic figures of the day.

In another passage Zola describes the work of an engine crew on the footplate with a precision and detail that must surely have come from personal observation. The central character of the novel, the driver Jacques Lantier, and his fireman, Pecqueux,

Left: Calais Maritime about 1904 with a de Glehn—du Bousquet 4—4—0 compound on a boat-train.
Right: Crampton locomotive No 80, *Le Continent*, built for the Paris to Strasbourg Railway (later part of the Est system) in 1852, is displayed at the Gare de l'Est in Paris in 1939. The 'single pair of huge driving wheels' on the locomotive of the Ouest system which impressed Zola some 20 years later is already in evidence.

Top: De Glehn–du Bousquet compound Atlantic No 221.2657 of the Nord at Boulogne-sur-Mer Ville. Above: Introduced in 1908, the Nord four-cylinder compound 4–6–0s of class 3500 remained in service until the mid-1960s. No 3586 is at Calais in August 1935.

are working an express from Paris to Le Havre.

In analyzing Jacques Lantier's affection for his engine, Zola considers the mystery of how inanimate materials can come together to build not simply a machine but a personality:

'Like the other engines of the *Compagnie de l'Ouest* it bore the name as well as a number — *Lison*, a station in the Cotentin. But Jacques' affection had made a woman's name out of it, *La Lison*, and on his lips the name became a caress.

'For it was true. In the five years that he had driven *La Lison* he had come to love her. . . . She was gentle, obedient, easy to handle when starting a train, and a steady runner because she steamed well. People liked to say that if she started so easily it was something to do with the tires and, above all, the precise setting of the slide valves; similarly, if she was a good steamer and burned little fuel, that was due to the quality of the copper in the tubes and good design of the boiler. But he knew there was something else, for other engines built to exactly the same plans and assembled with equal care showed none of these qualities. Here there was a spirit, a mystery of manufacture, something hammered

into the metal by forging, diffused into every part by the workman's hands; the personality of the locomotive, its very life.'

This same elusive quality remained with the steam locomotive to the end. The engines Zola knew were simple-expansion machines, for compounding did not begin in France until later in the century. Compounding is a system for extracting maximum energy from the steam by expanding it down to a low pressure, much below that at which it normally escapes from the locomotive blastpipe. This has to be done in two stages; the high-pressure cylinders take steam direct from the boiler in the usual way, but instead of the steam being exhausted direct to the atmosphere it is fed to the steamchests of the low-pressure cylinders (or cylinder) and does more work in those cylinders before reaching the blastpipe.

The history of the French compound, which culminated after World War II, began with a 4–2–2–0 built for the Chemins de fer du Nord in 1885. Its design was a joint venture by Alfred de Glehn, Chief Engineer of the builders, the Société Alsacienne des Constructions Mécaniques (SACM), and Gaston du Bousquet, Chief Mechanical Engineer of the Nord. The wheel arrangement, with two uncoupled driving axles

Above: An earlier du Bousquet 4—6—0, class 230A, was also long-lived, No 3.181 having been photographed at the Gare du Nord in 1939.

powered individually by the high-pressure and low-pressure cylinders, was the same as that of one of the compound classes designed by Francis Webb for the London & North Western Railway in England, and a Webb compound of that type had in fact been bought by the Chemins de fer de l'Ouest in 1884. Both designs showed a tendency to slip when starting trains, but it was far more acute in the Webb engines, which were no more than a passing phase in the development of the British steam locomotive whereas the de Glehn-du Bousquet compound was the beginning of an era in France. Later compounds for the Nord, however, were 4—4—0s with coupled axles, and in 1900 the railway introduced a series of compound Atlantics which soon acquired widespread fame. Engines of the same design were bought by other railways in France, and one went to the Great Western Railway in England.

Soon the same compounding principle was applied in France to 4—6—0 locomotives, but the Nord Atlantics had a long and distinguished career. Various changes took place over the years. In later engines of the series the bogies wheelbase was lengthened and in 1912 they were superheated and the diameter of the high-pressure cylinders was increased. From 1930 some of the class were fitted with high-capacity tenders for making nonstop runs, such as Paris–Brussels. Up to World War II they could be seen on moderately loaded trains such as the 'Oiseau Bleu' and the 'Nord Express.' The Atlantics which finally worked these services were equipped with smoke deflectors and Lemaître blastpipes, somewhat to the detriment of their appearance. The engines could maintain 75 mph (120 kph) on the level with 448 US tons/400 UK tons/406 tonnes and on through services between Calais and the Mediterranean coast were known to recover as much as a 40-minute delay in leaving Calais with loads of between 180 and 225 US tons.

Like the other lines, the Nord advanced to the 4—6—0, putting its 3500 class with this wheel arrangement into traffic between 1908 and 1912. In January 1938, by which time they had become class 230D, there were still 149 in service. These were very versatile machines, and to this fact they owed their long lives, for when they were stepped down from the crack trains such as the 'Nord Express,' which they worked regularly before 1914, they acquitted themselves well on duties ranging from perishable freight running at express speed to the humblest miscellaneous goods. They could run at 75 mph (120 kph) with trains of 560 US tons or climb a 1-in-200 gradient with a load of between 1000 and 1120 US tons. The only material modification made to them was in their exhaust arrangements. Otherwise there were mainly changes in detail, such as the fitting of turbo-generators for lighting, lengthening of the cab roof, and alterations in the lateral control of the bogie. Schmidt superheaters and piston valves were fitted in the 1930s. Du Bousquet had thought of a mechanical stoker but did not put the idea into practice. The floor of the tender coal space was inclined, however, to feed the fuel forward toward the fireman. With coupled wheels of only 5 feet 9 inches (1753 mm) in diameter, the 3500s anticipated the later general-purpose locomotive at a time when classes for different types of traffic were still proliferating, and they survived into the period when the ability of small-wheeled engines to run at high speeds was becoming generally accepted. Du Bousquet had allowed for the high-piston speeds necessary with 5-foot 9-inch (1753-mm) wheels by an increase in the cross-section of the steam passages of 25 percent on the high pressure side and 30 percent on the low pressure compared with the Atlantics.

In 1912 the Nord went ahead to compound Pacifics. They had been preceded by two compound 4–6–4s which had been planned by du Bousquet to cope with heavier trains than the 4–6–0s but did not appear until after his death. For this reason they were sometimes called 'the two orphans' and no more were built. The design was aimed at hauling trains of 448 US tons/400 UK tons/406 tonnes on the level at 75 mph (120 kph) and to maintain 60 mph (97 kph) up gradients of 1-in-200, but they were long and cumbersome engines and it soon became apparent that the same performance could be obtained from a 4–6–2. Motive power shortage after World War I made it necessary to keep the 4–6–4s in service, but with restricted route availability. In 1937 one of them was sectioned for display at an exhibition in Paris and in this condition actually survived World War II.

The first Nord Pacifics were the 20 engines of 1912. They immediately showed their advantage over the Atlantics in pulling power and speed. Before World War I, one of them was recorded as accelerating a 37-US-ton/33-UK-ton/34-tonne train from 35 to 64.5 mph (56 to 103.8 kph) up ten miles (16.1 km) of 1-in-200, another maintained 72–73 mph (116–118 kph) on the level with 414 US tons/370 UK tons/376 tonnes, and a third climbed the 1-in-200 of Survilliers bank with the 'Nord Express' weighing 594 US tons/530 UK tons/538 tonnes at a minimum of 50 mph (81 kph), afterward maintaining 64.5 mph (103.8 kph) along the level.

Even while the first 20 Pacifics were under construction, however, designers were thinking of something larger for the future, when the axle-load restriction of 19 US tons/17 UK tons/17 tonnes might be lifted. Action in this direction was delayed by the war and it was 1923/4 before a new series appeared. By this time the main lines had been relaid and could take an axle-load of 20.7 US tons/18.5 UK tons/18.8 tonnes. This new batch of 40 engines soon earned the name of Les Supers and did notable work on express trains of between 675 and 785 US tons. Their employment on boat trains between Paris and the Channel ports of Boulogne and Calais made them familiar to many travellers outside France. Cylinders were larger than in the first Pacifics and there was ten percent more adhesion weight. Working pressure was 227 lb per square inch (15.9 kg/sq cm) as before but grate area was increased from 34.7 to 37.7 square feet (3.2 to 3.5 sq m). One of these engines hauled the 'Golden Arrow' on its inaugural run on 11 September 1926 when the load of nine Pullman cars and a van totalled 608 US tons/543 UK tons/552 tonnes. Other services at this period loaded regularly up to between 675 and 725 US tons and on occasions the Calais–Mediterranean Express with 14 vehicles weighed even more. With loads of this order the Supers ran easily on the level at the official maximum speed of 75 mph (120 kph) and were little perturbed by gradients. On one occasion a special train of 851 US tons/760 UK tons/772 tonnes was taken up the 1-in-200 of Survilliers bank at 53 mph (85 kph). But still better was to come from later developments of steam motive power.

The success of the French compound locomotive

Above: The Nord Pacifics built between 1922 and 1931 were known as Les Supers. No 3.1255, of the batch built in 1930/31, waits to leave the Gare du Nord with an express to Boulogne and Calais in 1939.
Left: The Etat also developed Pacifics and improved the breed by rebuilding in the 1930s. The 231D class No 606 heads an express to Le Havre near Bonnières sur Seine in SNCF days.
Right: Packages in the van appeal mutely for attention while the crew of 231D755 enjoy a chat after arrival at Cherbourg.

in the de Glehn/du Bousquet tradition is a tribute to the competence of the crews and the standard of technical training they received. The de Glehn compound had two regulators, one controlling the high-pressure and one the low-pressure cylinders, and an intercepting valve. For starting a train it was usual to open both regulators but to leave the intercepting valve shut. Live steam then entered all four cylinders.

The high- or low-pressure regulators could also be used alone with the intercepting valve shut; the engine then worked as a two-cylinder simple with one or the other pair of cylinders in action. This arrangement was suitable for maneuvering a light locomotive.

In normal running the driver closed the low-pressure regulator and opened the intercepting valve controlling the engine with the high-pressure regulator. In this condition the engine worked as a four-cylinder compound, the steam exhausted from the high-pressure cylinders passing to the low-pressure cylinders. If the low-pressure regulator was opened in this condition, live steam was admitted to the low-pressure steamchests raising the pressure there to a

Below: Impressed by Chapelon's rebuilding of a PO Pacific, the Nord ordered 20 rebuilds from the PO and had more locomotives built on similar lines by outside industry. These were the Chapelons Nords, class 231E. No 231E17 climbs out of Boulogne with a Paris–Calais train.
Above: Chapelon Nord No 231E44 waits at Calais Maritime to take the 'Golden Arrow' to Paris.
Above right: No 231E27 on shed at La Chapelle Depot, Paris.

Left: The 4–8–0 class, 240P, was another conversion on Chapelon principles from earlier PLM locomotives and was carried out in wartime in 1940. The engine illustrated is 240P12.
Below: K class Pacific No 231K37 is about to leave Brussels Midi with the 18.57 express to Paris Nord.

limit set by a safety valve. This was called 'reinforced compound' working and could be used to boost the effort for short periods when accelerating a train or climbing a gradient.

Added to the above possibilities was the fact that the driver had separate sets of valve gear for the high-pressure and low-pressure cylinders under his control. Getting the best out of such a locomotive required skill and judgment, with quick interpretation of the readings given by the instruments in the cab. All this was forthcoming in full measure. It meant, of course, that the engine crews had to be supported by expertise and dedication on the part of the maintenance staff.

The Paris, Lyons & Mediterranean Railway (PLM) was another early and ardent supporter of compounding. In fact its curious 4–4–0s of 1894, the Machines à bec with their wedge-shaped smokebox doors intended to reduce wind resistance, were of the same type. Compounding on the PLM did not follow the de Glehn/du Bousquet pattern. There was no separate adjustment of the high- and low-pressure valve gear and no provision for simple working. When starting, however, the driver could operate a valve which increased the pressure in the low-pressure cylinders.

In 1909 the PLM introduced two Pacifics, one a saturated steam simple and the other a superheated compound. Comparative trials showed the superiority of the compound in fuel consumption so that arrangement was adopted for the future. By the early 1930s the PLM had 371 engines of substantially the same Pacific design in service and had converted a number of simple Pacifics to compound working.

A series of improvements was made in the PLM Pacifics over the years. Rebuilding of one machine with an improved steam circuit laid the foundation for the PLM 231 class, the most powerful of the PLM Pacifics, capable of 3200 indicated horsepower at 75 mph (120 kph). Similar modifications were made in other earlier Pacifics, producing classes 231G and 231K.

In the 1920s the Pacifics were having difficulty in accelerating quickly with heavy trains if delayed on severe gradients. A 4–8–2 design was therefore introduced to provide greater adhesion, the prototype appearing in 1925. The first of the production series appeared in 1927 and by 1932 the class totalled 145. Their work was mainly on the Laroche–Dijon and Marseilles–Nice sections of the PLM main line.

A similar step was taken by the Chemins de fer de l'Est when it needed more power for working heavier trains over the 1-in-167 gradients of the main line from Paris to Belfort. The first Est 4–8–2, in fact, came out a month or so before the PLM prototype and was the first locomotive with the 4–8–2 (Mountain) wheel arrangement in Europe. It had a long trial period during which changes were made in cylinder dimensions and grate area, and experiments with smoke deflectors were carried out. In 1930 it was on show at the Liège exhibition and it was not until a year later that deliveries of the production version began. These 40 new engines were similar to the prototype except that they had a shorter smokebox and a further increase in grate area. The class worked on the Paris–Nancy line as well as the Paris–Belfort, tackling its long gradients at 1-in-125, one of which extends for over eight miles (12.8 km). After further modifications in 1933 which included an improved steam circuit, higher superheat and feedwater heating, the Est 'Mountains' showed themselves able to

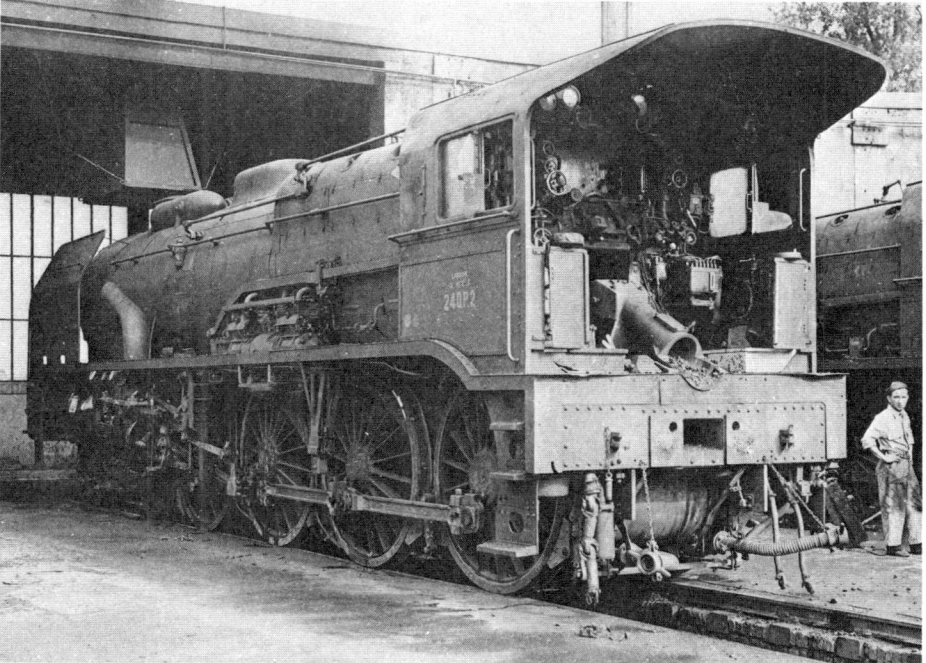

haul a 728 US tons/650 UK tons/660 tonnes train on the level at 56 mph (90.1 kph) and to take 616 US tons/550 UK tons/559 tonnes up 1-in-125 at 37 mph (60 kph).

In the 1930s the Chemins de fer de l'Etat, once a somewhat somnolent concern, underwent vigorous modernization. In updating its motive power it acquired some 4–8–2s similar to those on the Est but also rebuilt some of its Pacifics. Rebuilding was much in the air in those days. It had begun with the work of André Chapelon on the Paris–Orleans (later PO–Midi) Railway in 1929. A Pacific locomotive had been built for the company in 1907 to work over the heavily graded lines in the Massif Central, and other PO Pacifics followed, but their performance proved little better than that of the Atlantics which had preceded them.

Chapelon set out to find the reason why. This was no mere juggling with dimensions in the hope of hitting on a magic formula but a thoroughgoing application of thermodynamic principles to which he

Top: Modification and modernization of earlier PLM Pacifics produced classes G and K, both of which in course of time worked over all Regions of the SNCF. Pacific 231G519 arrives at Yvetot with a morning express from Le Havre to Paris in May 1964. Above: This footplate view of a 240P shows the pipe through which coal was fed by a rotating screw into the mechanical stoker.

taneous displacement of the products of combustion. These fluids are in frictional contact with the surfaces that guide them, but while the energy so expended is useful in the case of the combustion gases, since the coefficient of transmission of heat by convection depends on the intensity of this friction, the same is not the case with steam. Any loss of pressure therein which does not produce external work, that is, which does not act on the pistons, constitutes a loss, by irreversibility which is inadmissible in the Carnot cycle.'

Among the best known products of Chapelon's work outside the PO Railway were the Pacifics on the Chemins de fer du Nord known as the Chapelons Nords. In 1933 the Nord tested a rebuilt PO Pacific against one of its own Pacifics and certain other locomotives on the main line between Paris and Calais. Chapelon's product proved so superior in power output to the Nord Pacific that the Nord ordered 20 rebuilt Pacifics from the PO company and had 28 similar locomotives built by the locomotive industry. The first were in service in 1934, inaugurating the famous 231E class. Many exploits of the Chapelons Nords have been recorded but one which is little known occurred as late as 1965 during tests of the overhead contact system for the Paris–Lille electrification. A test train was made up consisting of an electric locomotive which was propelled 'dead,' but with pantograph raised, by a 231E Pacific. A laboratory vehicle and an ordinary vehicle behind the steam locomotive made up a load of 252 US tons/225 UK tons/229 tonnes. Three Pacifics were involved and more than 70 return trips were made between Aulnoye and Valenciennes, in the course of which maximum speeds of between 100 and 105 mph (161 and 169 kph) were reached at Le Quesnoy.

A correspondent of the English technical weekly *The Engineer* described a number of runs he made on class 231E Pacifics in the 1960s. He was impressed by the equipment of the cabs:

'Everything necessary for efficient and economical operation is there; the numerous gauges which are for use, not ornament – they are

**Above: The PLM introduced 4–8–2s in 1927 for duties which were getting beyond the capabilities of the Pacifics in some respects, and by 1932 had 145 of the type in service. A PLM 4–8–2 enters Toulon with a train from Marseilles in 1938.**

**Below: More 4–8–2s were built by the SNCF between 1948 and 1952 for the main line from Paris to Marseilles, but were confined to the Dijon–Marseilles section because of electrification between Paris and Dijon. Their territory diminished as 'the wires' extended southward, and they were later sent to other Regions. One of this impressive series is caught by the camera at speed.**

had devoted deep thought. The result was a complete redesign of the steam circuit of Pacific No 3566, involving enlarged and 'streamlined' steam passages, better steam flow through the valves, higher superheat and improved draft arrangements. Tested in heavy express traffic after this treatment, No 3556 showed an increase in maximum output of no less than 50 percent and better thermal efficiency. On one occasion the locomotive took a train of 635 US tons/567 UK tons/576 tonnes over the 70.1 miles (112.8 km) from Poitiers to Angoulême in 62.75 minutes. Similar success attended Chapelon's rebuilding of PO 4–8–0 locomotives.

Chapelon's philosophy of steam locomotive design can be studied in his book, *La Locomotive à Vapeur*, first published in 1938. It is a solid work of 900 pages and it is more often referred to with reverence than it is actually read or quoted. Much of it is highly detailed discussion of advanced physics which is usually preceded by a simple statement of what the author is about to demonstrate. Here is his introduction to the all-important subject of the steam circuit:

'The flow of the driving fluid results in simul-

watched closely and the engine is handled accordingly. They indicate superheater temperature, steamchest and receiver pressure, exhaust pressure, smokebox vacuum, pyrometer. They tell the crew what is happening all over the engine — there is no guesswork about anything.'

Although the high-pressure and low-pressure valve gears were independently adjustable it became the usual practice to lock the controls together and operate them as one. Separate adjustment might be used in special circumstances such as maintaining speed with a heavy train on a rising gradient. At one time there had been a theory among the crews that engines would run better with a long low-pressure cut-off. Chapelon discouraged the practice in the section of his book dealing with driving practice, characteristically by drawing attention to the message of the cab instruments. If the driver watched their readings while running with a long low-pressure cut-off, he would see a higher exhaust pressure and smokebox vacuum, two infallible indications of more steam entering the cylinders. But this was an artificial way of getting more steam in. He should try the experiment of lengthening the high-pressure cut-off while keeping the low-pressure cut-off short. Then he would find similar readings to before, but with the engine running still better. Chapelon advocated keeping the two cut-offs approximately the same, especially on locomotives with an improved circuit and therefore an in-built safeguard against wiredrawing. Ill-considered use of the valve gear controls could undo all the designer's work in planning the machine proportions and dimensions.

On his passenger train journeys with 231Es the correspondent of *The Engineer* noticed no use of the facility for admitting live steam to the low-pressure cylinders for boosting effort. This was done, however, when working freights on steeply graded routes at speeds in the 10- to 15-mph (16- to 24-kph) range, when it might continue for half-an-hour or more. The same commentator noted the smooth operation of the two regulators, which he considered contributed to the rarity of slipping, for during all the thousands of miles he had travelled on French railways he had seen this occur less than half a dozen times. The smooth riding of the 231Es impressed him in particular: 'It is delightful to ride them and feel their sewing machine smoothness noting the nonexistent opposing action between engine and tender — at times I have observed this less than an inch . . . engine and tender might have been glued together.'

These comments were made in the last years of French steam and in very different circumstances from those in which Chapelon had begun his work. On 1 January 1938 the French main-line railways had come together in the Société Nationale des Chemins de fer Français (SNCF).

A step toward rationalizing the motive power and rolling-stock policy of the French railways had been taken as early as 1919 by setting up the Office Central d'Etudes de Matériel (OCEM), but limited finance restricted its powers. It was to the OCEM, however, that the Nord turned in the 1930s for new designs of heavy passenger locomotives as successors to the Chapelons Nords, stipulating that they should follow the Chapelon doctrines that had proved so successful in that case. The result was a series of 4—6—4 express passenger engines comprising an experimental turbine design, three three-cylinder simples and four four-cylinder compounds (SNCF classes 232Q, 232R and 232S respectively). Monsieur de Caso of OCEM was responsible for the design and he was imbued with the Chapelon principles. The class appeared at the beginning of World War II.

Chapelon's last design for the PO Railway before it merged with the SNCF was an experimental 2—12—0 compound for heavy freight with four low-pressure and two high-pressure cylinders. Nominally a conversion of an existing 2—10—0, it was so completely rebuilt as to be really a new locomotive. The design first took shape in 1936 and was inherited by the SNCF on its formation two years later. Work was delayed by the war and locomotive trials did not begin until 1948. By that time steam on the SNCF was in eclipse. Chapelon retired in 1953 and his 12-coupler was scrapped in 1955. It had been a

Below: It is June 1939 and already the troop trains are rolling. Est 4—8—2 No 241—008 waits at the Gare de l'Est for departure to 'somewhere on the frontier.'

Left: De Caso's 4—6—4 compound 232U—1 has arrived at the Gare du Nord with an evening express from Belgium. This locomotive was built as a replacement for a 4—6—4 turbine locomotive which was scrapped after the war. Right: The eight 4—6—4s sanctioned before the war by the SNCF comprised the turbine 232Q1, three three-cylinder simples of class 232R, and four four-cylinder compounds of class 232S, built in the war years. No 002 of the 232S class is seen in this picture.

radical departure from the conventional compound layout. To provide the high tractive effort required for heavy goods working, the high-pressure cylinders had to be of large diameter, which meant that the low-pressure cylinders were larger than anything used before, too big in fact to go between the frames. Two were therefore placed outside, and two inside the frames, one pair driving the second and the other the third coupled axle. This arrangement is not readily apparent in photographs of the locomotive because of the steam jacketing of the cylinders (which included the high-pressure pair) to reduce losses by compensation. The high-pressure cylinders were between the frames near the center of the locomotive and drove the fourth coupled axle.

In the war years utility had to be the watchword. At first, construction of existing types continued, but from 1942 the SNCF began placing in service a series of general-purpose 2—8—2s (class 141P) designed for a top speed of 65 mph (105 kph) and of low adhesive weight for wide route availability. They were four cylinder compounds with linked high-pressure and low-pressure valve gears of the type favored by the PLM (now the Région Sud-Est) and performed well on the types of duty for which they were intended. Compounding was adopted for its proved economy in fuel consumption, which was foreseen as becoming a critical factor in the war years, but at the same time the relatively complicated mechanism of a compound was not an ideal choice for war conditions from the point of view of maintenance.

Had wartime destruction in France been less severe, the 141P class might have formed the nucleus of a large postwar standard general purpose fleet, with a new generation of locomotives for the fastest express duties. With the return of peace the turbine 4—6—4 of de Caso's prewar design was scrapped and replaced by a compound of the same wheel arrangement classified 232—U1. Here de Caso used PLM compounding practice, but with refinements. The locomotive started as a simple with 75 percent cut-off in the high-pressure cylinders and the low-pressure

cut-off advanced by a servo mechanism to 90 percent. The driver notched up in the usual way, with a partly opened regulator to reduce the risk of slipping, and when the high-pressure cylinders were cutting off at 55 percent the servo system notched up the low-pressure valve gear to the same extent; the locomotive then worked as a compound with the two sets of valve gear controlled together.

Chapelon had continued to work on designs for larger and more efficient steam locomotives. The opportunity to put his plans into practice came in 1946 when the SNCF sanctioned conversion of an Etat 4—8—2, which had been designed by the OCEM and was a somewhat doubtful performer, into a 4—8—4 on Chapelon's principles. This was the classic 242—A1, a three-cylinder compound capable of a maximum output of 5500 indicated horsepower. On trial runs it climbed the steep gradients to Blaisy Bas summit, north of Dijon, at between 60 and 70 mph (97 and 113 kph) with loads of over 896 US tons/ 800 UK tons/813 tonnes, and on one occasion on the Nord accelerated 874 US tons/780 UK tons/793 tonnes from a start at Creil to 72 mph (116 kph) at the summit of the 1-in-200 Survilliers bank. However plans for electrification of the former PLM and Nord main lines were already advanced. No 242—A1 was returned to the Etat (now the Region Ouest) where it had made its undistinguished start as a 4—8—2, and little further use was made of its new potential until it was withdrawn in 1960.

To return to the immediate postwar scene, the French locomotive works were in no condition to produce locomotives on the scale required in the period of reconstruction. Re-equipment of the SNCF after the war had to come partly from outside and so one saw the influx of the American built 2—8—2s of class 141R under the Marshall Plan. These were simple expansion engines, robust and easy to maintain; 1340 were ordered, but 16 went down in the transport ship *Bel Pamela* and one was lost during unloading in France. By 1947 the 1323 engines safely delivered could be seen at work all over France

**Above:** The 2–8–2 wheel arrangement was also used in tank locomotives for suburban services from St Lazare. Two three-cylinder locomotives of class 141T are on a spur line outside the terminus, with the Pont de l'Europe in the background, setting of the scene described by Zola and quoted at the beginning of this chapter.

on the widest possible variety of duties, from steel and coal trains in northeast France to the Blue Train on the Riviera. The last 141R 'dropped its fire' for the last time in 1974. Some of the class had run more than 1,240,000 miles (1,995,160 km) on the SNCF by the time they were withdrawn.

De Caso's 4–6–4 232–U1 survived to work the last steam train into the Gare du Nord on 30 September 1961. Train No 144 from Jeumont to Paris was also the last trip for the driver, Leprêtre. Crowds awaited the arrival and two bouquets were handed up to the footplate, one for Leprêtre and one for the locomotive, which, like him, was going into retirement. The occasion was recalled by Monsieur Jacques Vincent, shedmaster at the famous La Chapelle depot, who wrote to a friend:

> 'This memorable day was the end of steam at La Chapelle, the end of 116 years of coal, smoke, steam, very clean engines and a superb staff of men who were at one with their own beautiful machines. It was the March of Time, the Triumph of Progress, but for men such as ourselves it was not a wonderful day but a very sad one, and our hearts were heavy. We drank

champagne as if at a funeral rather than a baptism. If our lips smiled, our hearts were full of tears. We had lost the best of ourselves.'

The case for the displacement of steam was simple and had little to do with the capacity of the steam locomotive, which Chapelon had amply proved to be still capable of improvement. One crew per locomotive had been the rule. 'How these men know, love and nurse their engines!' wrote one enthusiastic observer. 'They often remain with an engine for years, getting to know it inside out and all its little tricks and whimsies, glad to do their own running repairs and working on them when general repairs are in hand.' But therein lay a weakness. The postwar authorities may have been doubtful over the continuing supply of men with such dedication. Even when they were to be had, the practice of *titularization* (the allocation of a crew to a particular engine) meant that the working hours of crew and engine were linked. Crewmen had 70 minutes preparatory work in the depot before taking their engine out, and another half-hour attending to it on their return.

The motive power departments were fully conscious of the problem and in some places the crew

Above: The 2–8–2s of class 141E were rebuilds of Est locomotives by the SNCF. Nos 141E566 and 430 leave St Cecile with a heavy train.

rosters were planned to give very high mileages. At Tours in 1934 some Pacific crews were running 254 miles (408.8 km) a day in a 12-day stint which included a rest period at Bordeaux followed by a duty of 338 miles (543.9 km) which landed them up at Nantes for another rest period away from home. Sometimes two crews were allotted to an engine, which could thus be kept on the road while either crew was off duty, but the benefits in utilization were small. Only a few classes of locomotive in those days were suitable for full common use, and that practice did not become general until the arrival of the postwar 141Rs. It was then extended to certain other classes, and the average daily engine-miles averaged over the whole steam fleet, which had long hovered between 50 and 60 miles (80.4 and 96.5 km) eventually reached 75 miles (120.7 km).

Chapelon's arguments for steam in his book were the arguments of an engineer rather than an operator. He quotes better sustained tractive effort at speed in a steam locomotive than in the diesel. In fact, he does not wholly concede the role of the diesel even as a shunting unit, but envisages a completely automatic oil-fired steam shunter which could be driven by one man. He calculates load hauled per indicated horse-power and shows that while for the private car and the truck the figures are 46.3 lb and 90.4 lb (21 kg and 41 kg) respectively, for the passenger train they are 881.8 lb (400 kg) and for the freight train 1411 lb (640 kg).

In a reference to his own initial success with the PO rebuilds, he quotes an increase in power/weight ratio measured at the cylinders from 23.7 hp/ton to 36 hp/ton, for an increase in locomotive weight of less than ten UK tons. He was optimistic about the future of the high-speed train, foreseeing average speeds 'between 80 and 90 mph (129 and 145 kph) or even more' which he thought, given the comfort, safety and convenience of rail travel, would be enough to outweigh the advantages of the private car or even the airplane.

It has been claimed that Chapelon's final 4–8–4 was quietly pushed into a corner because its prowess was embarrassing to the authorities when they had decided on far-reaching main-line electrification. But power *per se* had become a quality of less significance to the operators than availability. Addressing a conference in 1952 Monsieur Louis Armand, General

Left: A DB rebuilt class 001 4–6–2 No 001 133–8 arrives at Cochem with a stopping train from Koblenz to Trier.
Right: German State Railways class 038 4–6–0 (Prussian P8) climbs past Ehlenbogen with a passenger train for Freudenstapt.
Below: East German steam. One of the DR's fine 01 class Pacifics, beautifully polished with a Hamburg–Berlin express in 1970.

Manager of the SNCF, crystallized current thinking when he remarked that the American manufacturers of diesels were basing their publicity not on maximum speed or engine horsepower, but simply on the fact that their machines would be more productive than anything known previously and would run the greatest number of miles a day. In France electric locomotives were already covering 436 miles (701.7 km) a day on the Paris–Dijon section of the PLM main line and some had reached 620 miles (997.8 km) hauling trains of 896 US tons/800 UK tons/813 tonnes. Chapelon himself had stressed the need for research, urging that the railway should not be allowed to become like an old house which its owners neglected because they disliked change, or were skeptical of proposed improvements. Now the period

of change had begun, and with it the running down of the form of traction to which he had devoted his career.

The Chapelon principles remained to the last, with some modifications. The final Chapelon was the famous 241P 4–8–2 of 1948 of which 35 were built. This had driving wheels of 6 feet 6.75 inches (2000 mm), a grate area of 53.8 square feet (5.0 sq m), axle-load of 22 US tons/20 UK tons/20 tonnes, total weight 144 US tons/129 UK tons/132 tonnes and capable of developing nearly 5000 horsepower. Though a few other locomotive designs and modifications appeared afterward, the 241Ps provided a suitable memorial to Chapelon and enabled the curtains to be drawn slowly on French steam to justified applause.

Below left: The class 141P 2–8–2 four-cylinder compounds were built between 1942 and 1949. No 141P 198 is the background to a conversation piece at Quimper in the last few moments before the 'off.' Below right: The postwar SNCF was re-equipped with 2–8–2s built in the United States, the very numerous class 141R, to be seen all over the system on duties of all kinds. No 141R772, an oil-burner, waits to move off shed at Sotteville Depot, Rouen.

Right: The whole world of steam, glowing in the twilight that was well advanced by 1960, lives in this picture of a 141R restarting a heavy fright near St Gerand-Mogret.

Left: French Railways No 141P198 2–8–2 at Quimper with an express for Paris in 1963.
Below left: East meets West. Czech State Railways 2–10–0 No 556 arrives at Schirning in West Germany with the Prague–Paris 'Zpadni Express.' The 2–10–0 has only come across the border from Cheb.
Right: Historic train. Swiss Central Bahn Engerth type 0–4–6T No 28 *Genf* (built in 1858) climbs the old Hauenstein line on the 120th Anniversary of the opening, August 1978.

# 6. Southern European Steam

In the 1930s the 'Rome Express' ranked second only to the 'Orient' and the 'Simplon–Orient' in its appeal to writers of fiction and producers of films. Its route from France into Italy was historic. The Romans built a military road across the Mont Cenis pass, and when the Emperor Constantine had to hasten south from Gaul to suppress a usurper at home, that was the route he took, leading his troops 'with such active diligence that he descended into the Plain of Piedmont before the court of Maxilenus had received any certain intelligence of his departure from the banks of the Rhine.' Centuries later a railway climbed through the Maurienne Alps on the French side and burrowed under the pass in the Mont Cenis Tunnel.

The 'Rome Express' ran for the first time in 1897 as a through train from Calais. Later it started from Paris, where a portion from Calais was attached. In the middle 1930s the Calais portion consisted of through coaches for Rome and Florence which were worked to Paris Gare du Nord on an ordinary train and then taken round by the Ceinture to the Gare de Lyon. For many years the 'Rome Express' was first class only and remained so when new rolling stock was introduced in 1930. The new sleeping cars provided six double-berth and four single-berth compartments

each. A year later the double-berth compartments were made second class and the train became available to both classes.

A traveller on the 'Rome Express' in the mid-1930s left the Gare de Lyon at 2025 hours and would probably have been unaware of the PLM Pacific coming off at Culoz in the night hours to be replaced by an electric locomotive. Electric traction continued from the Italian frontier at Nodane right down to Livorno, but steam banking assistance might be provided out of Alessandria where the line climbed out of the Plain of Lombardy to cross the mountains between there and the coast at Genoa.

Steam took charge at Livorno for the rest of the journey to Rome, and as a rule the train was double-headed by two class 685 2–6–2s. The 2–6–2 tender locomotive for express work was a characteristic of the Italian railways which could be traced back to 1907, two years after the formation of the Italian State Railways by fusion of the three previous major independent systems. The first example, class 6–8–0, was a four-cylinder compound on the Plancher system in which the two high-pressure cylinders were inside and outside the frames on one side of the locomotive while the two low-pressure cylinders were arranged

Left: The class 625 2–6–0, dating from the first decade of the century, exhibits the typical Italian feature of inside cylinders with outside valve gear.

**Above: The characteristic Italian main line 2–6–2. FS No 685.172 leaves Cremona with the 12.56 train for Milan on 31 May 1967.**

similarly on the other side. Both cylinders in each group had a common steamchest with one piston valve admitting steam to both cylinders. The valves were driven by outside Walschaerts gear. On the first movement of the regulator, live steam was admitted to all cylinders, but as it was opened further the locomotive worked as a compound.

As built, the class 680 locomotives were not superheated, but after a trial of superheating in two of them, 36 of the class were converted similarly and reclassified as class 681. In seven locomotives the ratio of the high-pressure to the low-pressure cylinder dimensions was altered and these became class 682.

In the next new design of 2–6–2s, class 685, the State Railways dropped compounding and chose a four-cylinder simple with superheated steam. There was much in common with the superheated 680s, and the same arrangement of a common steamchest

and piston valve for the two cylinders on each side of the locomotive was retained in the simple locomotive. The first of the class were supplied by Breda in 1912. Four locomotives were equipped with Caprotti valve gear in 1924 and reclassified as class 686. Results were satisfactory and 30 new Caprotti engines of class 686 were built in 1926/27. In 1930, however, all the Caprotti engines, rebuilds and new, were taken back into class 685. Five of them were rebuilt in 1940 with Franco–Crosti boilers, their numbers at first taking a letter 'S' prefix but they were later designated class 683.

The Italian 2–8–2s underwent numerous changes during their working life, the most fundamental being the rebuilding of 680 class No 110 as a turbine locomotive in 1930. An early experiment with turbine propulsion had been made in Italy in 1908 with the conversion of an 0–6–0 shunting locomotive to

Right: Italian State Railways 2–6–2 locomotive at Táranto.

Below: Italian branch line. Steam is spasmodic in Italy with very little on the active list. This class 625 2–6–0 is one of those still in use, some with Crosti boilers. This is No 625.042 with an enthusiasts' excursion in 1974.

Bottom: Once the pride of Calais Depot, this SNCF class 231K Pacific is now part of the collection of preserved steam engines at Steamtown Museum, Carnforth.

122

geared turbine drive to the design of Professor Guisseppe Belluzzo. No condenser was used, the object being to test the mechanical suitability of a turbine drive rather than its economics. This pioneer machine worked for some 12 years. The 1930 conversion, however, did not get beyond a few trial runs on which a speed of 80 mph (129 kph) was reached. The experiment was not judged a success and the locomotive was restored to its original form, remaining in service until 1969.

Professor Belluzzo was still interested in turbine locomotives in the 1930s and was behind the building by Breda in 1931 of an experimental 2–8–2 with turbine drive and a condenser. In contrast with previous condensing turbine locomotives have a separate tender, in this design all the equipment – turbines, condenser and heat exchanger – was carried on the engine itself. The turbine group, consisting of high – and intermediate – pressure turbines on one side of the locomotive and two low-pressure turbines on the other side, was positioned between the second

and third coupled axles, leaving the area in front of the smokebox free for the heat-exchanger. The condenser was between the smokebox and the first coupled axle. The drive from the turbine shafts was taken through gears and a jackshaft to the coupling rods. After a few trial runs the project was abandoned.

The visitor to Italy in the 1930s who saw one of the turbine locomotives would have been fortunate, but he might well have been surprised to see one of the cab-at-front 4–6–0s of class 670 which dated from 1900 but were still at work in 1936. They were built for the Rede Adriatica system and taken over by the State Railways. At first sight one would have thought that a class 670 was an 0–6–4 tank engine running bunker first and towing a small tank wagon but closer inspection would show the 'bunker' to be a cab and the tank wagon a tender carrying water supplies. Coal was carried in two bunkers alongside the firebox which had the appearance of the water tanks in a conventional side-tank engine. Early tests were carried out on a section of the PLM in France,

**Above: Class 940 2–8–2T, No 940.050, leaves a way-side station with an evening local train from Lecco to Como. This class was a tank version of the class 740 2–6–0 of 1911.**
**Above right: Class 625 No 625.042 heads an enthusiasts' special at Lagonegro. These engines worked some of the last regular steam passenger trains in Italy, between Verona and Modena.**
**Right: An enthusiasts' special headed by a class 625 2–6–0 winds its way through a hilly landscape.**

using a French dynamometer car, and a maximum speed of 78.3 mph (126 kph) was recorded with a train weighing 146 US tons/130 UK tons/132 tonnes. In their early days they had been regarded as an express locomotive and the cab had a rounded front to reduce wind resistance at speed. The class numbered 43 locomotives, the last of which were delivered after the formation of the State Railways. At the end of their days they could be seen working local passenger trains out of Milan and shunting in the carriage sidings; by that time they looked extremely shabby but were still apparently capable of useful work.

To return to the 2–6–2s, their axle-load was 15 or 16 UK tons, according to class, which enabled them to be used on nearly all the main routes. For the most part, however, they worked on the less hilly lines in central and northern Italy. The last survivors were members of class 685, which ended their days from the middle 1960s on local passenger and freight duties on secondary lines, some of them going to Sicily.

Those who watched the twilight of Italian steam will also remember the inside-cylinder 2–6–0s with outside valves and Walschaerts valve gear. Some of the 2–8–0s were similar. Pacifics were built from 1911 but were sluggish performers. A project for a more modern three-cylinder simple Pacific with three sets of valve gear was mooted in the 1920s but did not come to fruition. At the same period a series of large 2–8–2s was introduced. These were four-cylinder compounds with a conventional cylinder arrangement, the low-pressure cylinders being out-

Above far left: Italian State Railways class 940 2–8–2T No 940.050 heads a Lecco-to-Como train between Civate and Sala al Barro Galbiate.
Above left: A southbound freight double headed by RENFE 241F 4–8–2s climbs toward Bujedo on the Miranda de Ebro-to-Burgos line.

Above: Portugal's CP 4–6–0 No 281 arrives at Tua with a freight bound for Porto.
Below: Spanish local. RENFE 4–8–2 No 241F 4065 approaches San Felices beside the river Ebro with a stopping train from Logrno to Miranda de Ebro.

side and the high-pressure inside. As in the Pacifics, the steam circuit was not conducive to free flow and the engines gradually retired to the south of the country where less arduous duties were to be found.

Perhaps Italy's most important contribution to the steam locomotive was the Caprotti valve gear, but even here the native product did not progress to the same extent as the corresponding gear built abroad under license. Main-line electrification came early to Italy, which had ample water power but no coal of its own. In these circumstances less effort was devoted to steam locomotives development than might otherwise have been the case. Even so, the apparent neglect of lessons to be learned from the steam practice in neighboring countries remains a surprising and not wholly explained aspect of Italian railway history.

The late 1970s saw the restoration of a little-known direct rail link between Italy and France. The first move came from the Italian side with the proposal for a line from Cuneo to Ventimiglia, serving Nice by a branch from Breil. By 1900 they had built a line across the Col di Tenda and reached Vievola on its southern slope. Long discussions with France followed, for the next stage of construction down the valley would cross and recross the frontier. It was finally agreed that the Italians should continue their line from Vievola, via Breil, to Ventimiglia, while the French would build a connecting line from Nice to Breil.

Work was delayed by World War I, and although the section from Ventimiglia to Breil was completed in 1921, the Nice–Breil branch was not ready until 1928. On 30 October 1928 the work was completed

and there was through communication from Nice to Cuneo. French and Italian inaugural trains, bedecked with flags, met in Breil station.

A few international services were instituted over the new route, which reduced the distance by rail from Nice to Turin from 180.2 miles (290 km) via Savona to 137.3 miles (220.9 km). The Italians worked their services at first with 0–10–0 locomotives of class 471 but replaced them later with the more powerful 2–8–2 tank engines of class 940. The PLM began its services with the few 4–6–0s of class 230C–1 to 230C–170 which were shed at Nice Saint Roch. Some 4–8–0s were sent specially from Alès later and worked on the line for a few months, to be followed by 4–6–4 tanks of the classes working coastal services. From 1930 the workings were largely in the hands of 4–8–4 tanks class 242T–1 to 242T–120, and these continued to be employed on the Nice–Breil section of the line until 1956–57, when they were succeeded by the 2–8–2s of class 141R. Between 1930 and 1935 the Italians electrified the route from Cuneo to Ventimiglia.

When Italy entered World War II in 1940 some of the works at the southern end of the line were destroyed by the French Army but were later restored and freight traffic to Italy and Germany continued. After the Allied landing in Provence on 15 August 1944 there was further bomb damage but the major destruction occurred in April 1945 during the German retreat and put the section from Breil to Vievola completely out of action. It remained derelict for many years and reconstruction was not put in hand until 1976. On 19 January 1979 the last fish-

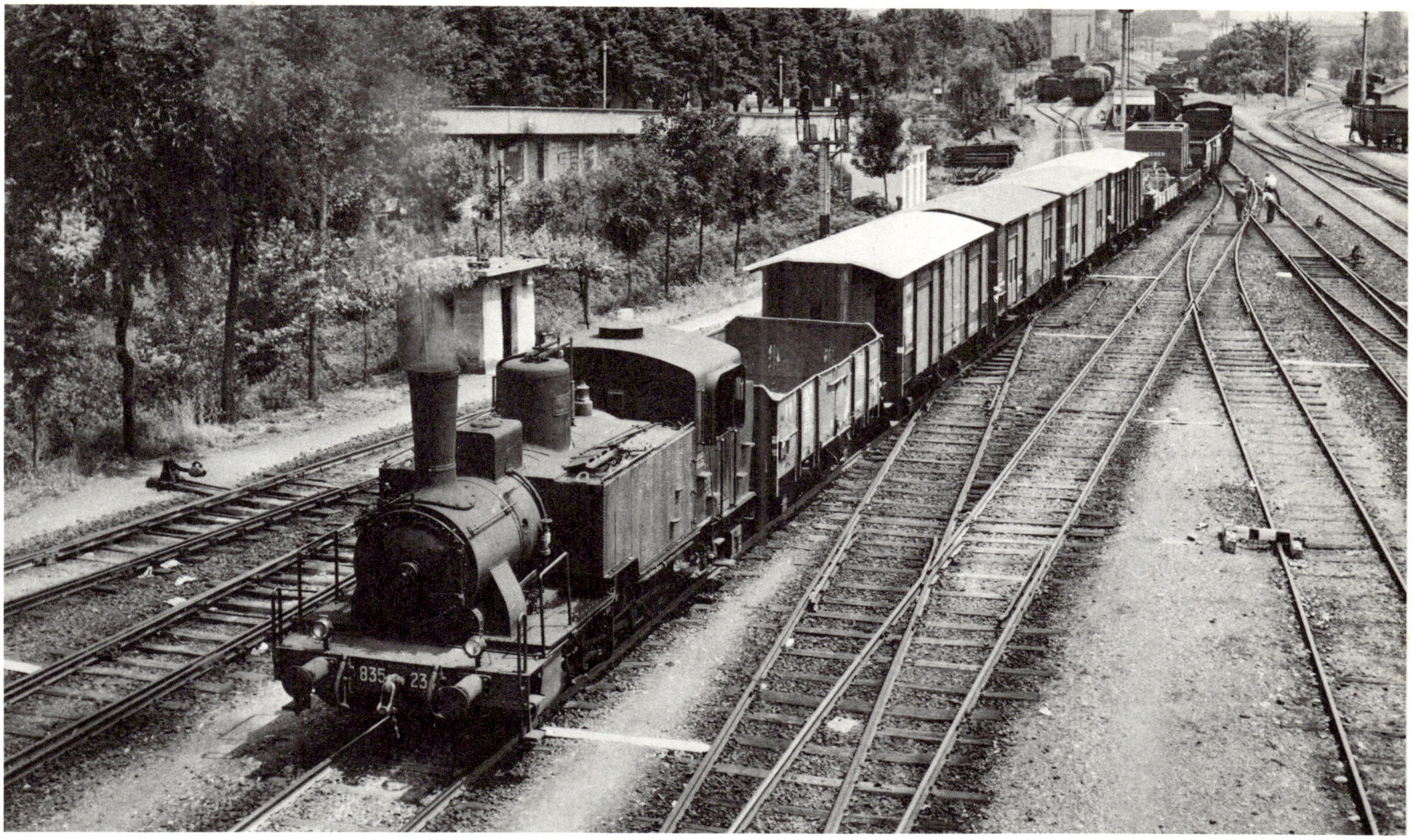

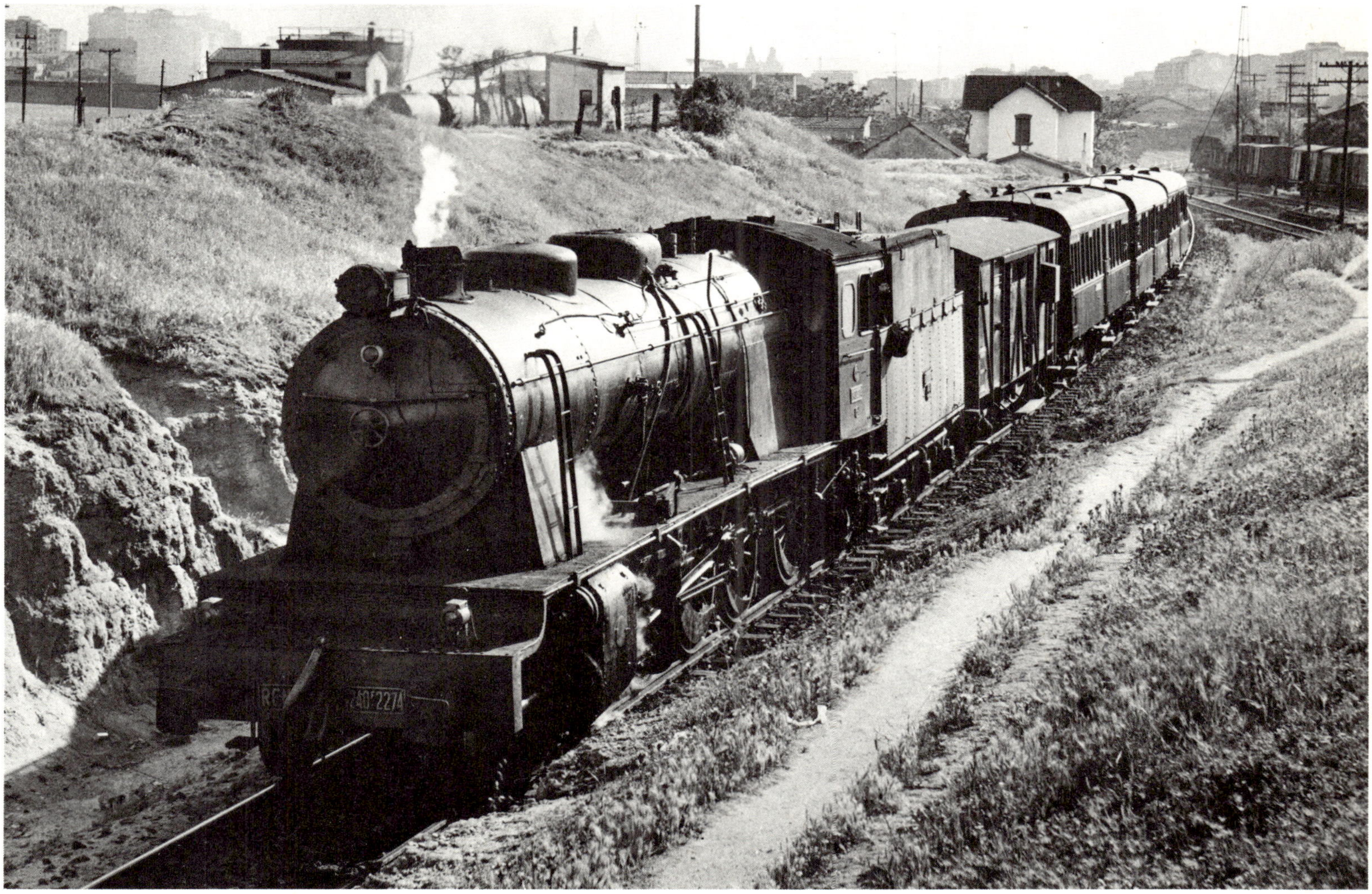

plate was bolted home in Breil station, re-establishing a through route from Italy to France via the Col di Tenda.

Spain, like Italy, acquired new rail links with France in the 1920s, although the 5-foot 6-inch (1.6-m) gauge of the Spanish Railways prevented through running. One of these lesser-known routes was opened in 1928 from Bedous on the French side of the Pyrenees to Jaca in Spain, giving a shorter journey from Pau to Zaragoza. It was a formidable line for the steam locomotives employed by both administrations, rising 2662 feet (811.4 m) from Bedous into the mountains in a distance of about 18 miles (29 km). The average gradient was around 1-in-35 and the steepest section was 1-in-23. The frontier was crossed in the Somport Tunnel, five miles (eight km) long; the line emerged at Canfranc, three miles (five km) inside Spain. From here a new line some 16 miles (25.7 km) long was built to Jaca on the existing Spanish network, dropping through 1300 feet (396 m) with an average gradient of 1-in-65. The section from Bedous is now closed and a bus service has been substituted, but RENFE railcars run between Canfranc and Zaragoza.

The other new link between France and Spain,

Above: Even the massive 'Mountains' were sometimes dominated by the craggy Spanish landscape, as in this scene near Pancorbo in 1968.
Above left: The 'Mountain' (4–8–2) wheel arrangement was first seen in Spain in the 1920s, following several 4–8–0 classes. It lasted until the end of steam. A 'Mountain' of class 241F No 2087 heads a passenger train in arid surroundings near Salamanca.
Left: Front-end assistance is provided by a 2–8–2 for a 'Mountain' leaving Pancorbo.

opened in 1929, provided a more direct journey from Toulouse to Barcelona than by the main line via Port Bou and Cerbère. New construction was necessary on the Spanish side from Ripoll to the frontier near Puigcerda. The frontier station was at La Tour de Carol on the French side, 33 miles (53.1 km) from Ripoll. Again the French section was the steeper, climbing from 4035 feet (1230 m) at La Tour de Carol to a summit of 5200 feet (1585 m) in the Puymorens Tunnel, 3.25 miles (5.23 km) long. Onward to a junction with an existing line at Ax les Thermes the new line descended steadily, and on the final section of 13 miles (21 km) from L'Hospitalet to Ax passed through 11 tunnels, one of them a spiral tunnel which dropped the line 200 feet (61 m) at an average gradient of 1-in-25. The route remains rail-operated throughout. First- and second-class sleeping cars are operated between Paris and La Tour de Carol by the SNCF.

In the period of maximum steam development elsewhere, Spain was in the midst of a civil war. When normal travel hours and tourism resumed after World War II visitors were impressed by the massive steam locomotives still coming into service in spite of much electrification work in parts of the country.

As in other countries of Europe, the 'big engine' era in Spain began in the latter half of the 1920s, although eight-coupled designs had long been in use because of the steeply graded main lines. Earlier in the century locomotives had been ordered from foreign builders but by 1920 a Spanish-built version of the Northern (Norte) Railway's 4–8–0 of 1912 was being produced.

The next step was to the Mountain (4–8–2) wheel arrangement, first seen in six passenger locomotives with eight-wheel bogie tenders built in Germany for the Norte in 1925. They were four-cylinder compounds of the de Glehn/du Bousquet type, but the width between the frames enabled all cylinders to be almost in line. Driving wheels were of just under 5 feet 9 inches (1753 mm) in diameter and the nominal top speed was 68.35 mph (110 kph). Later engines of the same class were built in Spain. One of these Norte 4–8–2s was rebuilt with a steam circuit incorporating Chapelon features. As a result of its improved performances 28 more locomotives incorporating similar modifications to the original design were built in the 1946–48 period.

The Madrid, Zaragoza & Alicante Railway (MZA) also introduced a 4–8–2 class in the middle 1920s

Right: A class of standard 2–8–2s was introduced by RENFE as late as 1953. One of these locomotives is on a passenger-working near San Felice.
Below: Huge and elusive as the Abominable Snowman, the RENFE 4–8–4s of class 242F became almost a legend in the last days of Spanish steam. The camera has caught and fixed No 2009 for all time in this scene near Bujedo in 1968.

Above: Class 141F 2–8–2 No 2327 approaches Haro with the 18.15 Miranda de Ebro-to-Casetas train on 15 May 1968.
Above right: RENFE used the boiler of its 4–8–2s in a 2–10–2 heavy freight series. No 151.3112 of this class heads a southbound freight through Palencia, on the Northern main line from Oveido and Leon to Madrid.

Above: A short freight on
the Portuguese Railways
near San Mameda de Tua
is headed by an outside-
cylinder locomotive characterized by a simplicity of
line rarely seen on the
Continent.
Right: Another 4–6–0 of
the same class is on a
freight working near Tua.
Above far right: A Portu-
guese example of the classic
inside-cylinder 4–6–0
outline.
Far right: Broad-gauge
2–8–4T No 0181 arrives at
Regua with a freight train
from Porto in May 1968.

but these were two-cylinder simples and were built in Spain from the outset. Driving-wheel diameter was the same as in the *Norte* class. In 1939 the MZA ventured into streamlining with a further batch of generally similar 4—8—2s but with the high boiler pressure of 295 lb per square inch (20.74 kg/sq cm), which involved some novelties in the design of the cylinder and piston-rod packing. Streamlining seems to have been adopted for ostentation rather than utility for no speeds at which aerodynamics needed to be seriously considered were in prospect.

The Spanish National Railways (RENFE) were formed in 1941 and continued the construction of 4—8—2s using a larger boiler. The same larger boiler was used in a class of three-cylinder simple 2—10—2s for heavy coal traffic in the north of the country. As late as 1953 a standard design of 2—8—2 mixed traffic locomotive was introduced, of which the first 25 came from the works of the North British Locomotive Company Limited in Scotland. Further construction followed in Spain and eventually 232 of these reliable and versatile locomotives were in service. Ten 4—8—4s built in the country in 1955—56 were the climax of Spanish steam design, although the last steam locomotives built in Spain were Beyer-Garratts under license. The 4—8—4s were still at work in 1974, ending their days on heavy freight duties. Like all the Spanish eight-coupled classes they were of majestic build but these stood out from the others by reason of their green livery. Deceptively, they had that air of permanence peculiar to the steam locomotive, looking as if they would last as long as the rocky terrain through which they moved with massive dignity. Against those towering smokeboxes the waves of time must surely dash themselves in vain. Yet all this was an illusion.

Spain was the only country in Europe to use Garratts regularly in passenger service. They were of a 4—6—2- and 2—6—4-type built under license by Spanish firms for the Central of Aragon Railway and six were delivered in 1931, together with six of a 2—8—2+2—8—2 class for freight. The passenger engine was designed for the steeply graded main line from Zaragoza to Valencia via Caminreal, where it was required to haul trains of 336 US tons/300 UK tons/305 tonnes at up to 62 mph (100 kph) on the level and at up to 25 mph (40 kph) up gradients of 1-in-46, with curvature of 984 feet (300 m) radius. These engines remained on their home ground for some ten years after RENFE was formed and then were put on the coastal line between Taragona and Valencia for working the Barcelona—Sevilla express. The Garratts coped single-handed with 17-coach trains which had previously required double-heading on this section, where the train made frequent stops and faced gradients as steep as 1-in-75. They remained on this duty until diesels came on the scene in 1966—67.

The freight Garratts were of smaller proportions than the passenger class. They remained on the Old Central of Aragon line until it was dieselized in 1966—67 but under RENFE also worked from Valencia to La Encina. In 1961 the original half-dozen were supplemented by ten more, generally similar but built for oil-burning. The others were all converted to oil fuel in the course of their lives.

Another type of articulated locomotive seen in Spain was the Mallet. A number of 0—6—6—0 Mallets were built between 1906 and 1928 for work on heavily graded lines and were still active around

Valencia in the 1960s. The meter-gauge Ponferrada–Villablino Railway used Engerth type 'tender-tank' engines. These are sometimes classified as articulated because of their derivation. Engerth pursued the idea of the locomotive *Bavaria* which was the prize-winner in the Semmering Trials in Austria in 1851. The *Bavaria* had a 'power tender' with two coupled axles, the leading one chain-driven from the rear coupled axle of the locomotive. Engerth replaced the chain with a gear drive. To achieve this the leading axle of what had been a separate tender was brought forward until it was in front of the firebox. It was then so close to the rear coupled axle that the two remained virtually parallel on curves. The four-wheel tender had, in fact, become a trailing four-wheel bogie which carried both the rear end of the boiler and the fuel supplies. The gear drive gave much trouble and was eventually abandoned. Locomotives of a similar configuration continued to be built, however. Strictly speaking they are 'Modified' Engerths.

Railway development in Portugal took an unusual turn – a large privately owned railway took over the smaller State lines. The Beira Alta had been con-

Left: The diminutive
0–4–0T No 003 serves as
shed pilot at Porto main-
line shed.
Right: A contrast in coach-
ing styles near Porto.

Left: Swiss Federal class
C/5 2–100 No 2978
leaves Mellingen with a
steam special during the
celebration of 100 Years of
the State Railways in 1977.
The C/5 class was the most
powerful and numerous
steam class in Switzerland;
78 were built between
1913 and 1917.
Below: An ex-Swiss Federal
0–6–0T heads a mixed
train leaving Sursee for
Triengen on the Sursee–
Triengen Bahn in 1964.

structed largely with French capital and it was, therefore, not unnatural that this country should have received the lion's share of orders for locomotives at the beginning of the century. The de Glehn system remained popular even after German manufacturers had taken the lead in supplying engines. This was best exemplified by the excellent 4–8–0s which were used to haul the international train from Vilar Formoso to Pampilhosa. These 1931 locomotives had 5-foot 4.12-inch (1628-mm) diameter wheels, a grate area of 42.7 square feet (3.97 sq m) and an axle-load of 16.5 US tons/14.5 UK tons/14.7 tonnes with an overall weight of 96 US tons/86 UK tons/87.4 tonnes. De Glehn compounding was also represented in three 4–6–0 classes and in 4–6–2s with narrow fireboxes produced in 1924.

The closing years of steam in Portugal were typified by a lack of native engine production and a generality of types imported from several countries, including the United States, Germany, France, Spain and even Switzerland, a country not noted for its locomotive exports. These were 2–6–4 tanks which were built for the Lisbon suburban system to Swiss design and by Swiss builders.

# 7. Northwestern European Steam

The railways of Belgium tended to be overshadowed by their larger neighbors but the centenary in 1935 of the first line in the country, connecting Brussels with Malines, directed attention to an enterprising system with many interesting aspects. Unlike the course of events in most other countries, the Belgian railway network was not built up from a number of separate undertakings but was planned as a unified state system from the outset. The backbone was to be a trunk line from Ostend to the Prussian frontier via Malines and Liège, with branches from Malines southward to Brussels and northward to Antwerp. The first section to be completed ran from Malines to Brussels and was opened on 5 May 1835. It was the first railway in Continental Europe to be operated with steam traction. A century later Belgium had the greatest railway mileage in proportion to its area of any European country.

Locomotive practice in Belgium went through a number of phases. Visitors from Great Britain were often surprised on arriving at Ostend to see 4–4–0s and 4–6–0s with a strong resemblance to what they were used to at home. In 1897 a Caledonian Railway 4–4–0 of the 'Dunalastair' class, designed by J F McIntosh, had been shown at the Brussels Exhibition of that year. The Belgians were impressed and forthwith ordered five similar engines from the builder in Scotland. Further construction by Belgian firms to the same design followed in the early 1900s, and other McIntosh engines inspired a succession of Belgian 0–6–0s and 4–6–0s of unmistakeably Caledonian antecedents but adapted to the requirements of the country. In fact the Belgian engines in the McIntosh tradition, eventually totalling more than 750, outnumbered the corresponding classes in Scotland. They included a 4–4–2 tank engine, a wheel arrangement which Caledonian had not used, with strong McIntosh characteristics.

Steam locomotives have long lives and this generation of 'Scotsmen' could still be seen at work in the 1930s, although the passenger engines had long since been retired from the heavy international trains and those on the steeply graded line to Luxembourg. There were even hardy survivors from a still earlier period. An observer recalls seeing a line of Belpaire's 2–4–2 express engines of the late 1880s drowsing in a siding near Ans in 1930. Belpaire was the chief mechanical engineer of the Belgian State Railways and later Administrative President. He is best remembered internationally for his firebox design, developed to burn the cheaper grades of coal efficiently. His 2–4–2s were double-framed to support a firebox with an exceptionally wide grate, fed through two firedoors.

After the 'Scottish' phase in Belgian locomotive design, both local and French influences were seen. The first move toward higher power for passenger trains was a four-cylinder simple 4–6–0 with all cylinders driving the leading axle. The first of this class had a complicated Walschaerts motion in which

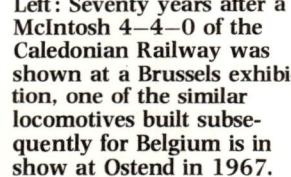

Left: Seventy years after a McIntosh 4–4–0 of the Caledonian Railway was shown at a Brussels exhibition, one of the similar locomotives built subsequently for Belgium is in show at Ostend in 1967.

Above: The 'Scottish' phase of Belgian locomotive practice was followed by various 4–6–0 classes. No 7051 is characteristic of the period.

Right: A double-framed 2–4–2 with a West Flanders train at Ostend in 1910.

the outside valve gear drove the *inside* valves through rocking shafts, while the inside valve spindles were extended at the other end to drive further rocking shafts which actuated the *outside* valves. Expert observers have been mystified by this inside-out arrangement and the reasons for its adoption. It was, in fact, dropped in favor of a more conventional system in later locomotives of the series. Contemporary with these engines was a de Glehn compound of the same wheel arrangement which was distinctly French-inspired in its general arrangement.

Then, in 1910, appeared the locomotive which epitomized the Belgian express train in the minds of railway enthusiasts (and illustrators of children's railway books) right up to the middle 1930s. This was the four-cylinder simple Pacific introduced by J B Flamme, and rebuilt with various improvements in 1922. Competent observers were impressed — even awed — by its appearance many years later. E S Cox of British Railways called the engines 'certainly the most extraordinary-looking Pacifics ever to have taken the rails . . . almost terrifying engines, and to see one approach with its vast capuchon chimney, and the formidable battlements of its inside cylinder covers, coupled with the muffled roar of its exhaust, was certainly something without parallel in any land.'

A basic characteristic of the design was the very large but relatively short boiler. The drive was divided, with the inside cylinders ahead of the outside and the latter actually in front of the smokebox,

so that the locomotive had an unusually spacious front platform on which the plating over the inside cylinders reared like an upper deck. There was, in fact, something of the aspect of a battleship viewed from the bows. In World War I a number of the locomotives were stored in France. Postwar rehabilitation included new superheater elements giving a larger heating surface, improved steam passages and a double blastpipe and chimney. The relatively short boiler avoided the loss of heat in the tubes at the smokebox and which reduced the steaming efficiency of some types where the boiler was of unusual length, as the North Eastern Railway Pacifics in England.

For much of their lives the engines retained the deep brass cap on the chimney which was characteristic of Belgian locomotives for many years. C Hamilton Ellis comments on the overwhelming appearance of a Flamme Pacific seen from a low platform typical of Belgian stations: 'As one loomed up in the Brussels twilight, for a moment or two the whole visible world seemed to be composed of a huge, roaring, brass-bound locomotive.'

The Flamme Pacifics lasted until the end of the steam era in Belgium, although they were displaced from the principal passenger services by a new Pacific series introduced in 1935. These were semistreamlined with four cylinders, but more conventionally disposed than in the Flamme arrangement. The cowling at the front was not unlike that of Gresley's 2–8–2 of the 'Cock o' the North' class built for the Edinburgh–Aberdeen line of the London & North

**Above:** A 4–6–0 No 64.130 clouds the outlook for lineside residents beside a rural station.
**Top right:** In abandoning the austere but dignified 'Scottish' tradition, Belgian steam locomotives tended to let boiler mountings and pipework run riot.
**Center right:** A Flamme Pacific enters Pepinster with a Verviers train.
**Right:** US (Baldwin)-built 4–6–0 No 40.014 heads a train of typical Belgian six-wheel stock forming the 14.44 to Oudenarde at Mons.

Eastern Railway in Scotland, the chimney being almost invisible in a side view of the locomotive. In that age of the Super Cinema, they inevitably came to be known as the 'Super Pacifics.'

The centenary year of the Belgian railways saw a general modernization of equipment and revision of internal train services to give faster city-to-city runs. A pointer to the future was electrification between Brussels and Antwerp, giving Belgium an early electric intercity service. The electric trains on this route had independent tracks. They were inaugurated on 23 April 1935 and on 5 May the King of Belgium made a formal trip over the line. Steam services on other lines were being worked to accelerated timings and operated with improved frequency by fixed-formation trains called *trains blocs*. Mile-a-minute runs increased steadily. Mileage covered at this speed expressed as a percentage of the total railway mileage in the country rose from 17 percent in 1935 to 49 percent in 1938. The peak was reached in May 1938 with the inauguration of lightweight high-speed trains between Brussels and Ostend hauled by streamlined Atlantic locomotives specially built for the service. They were allowed one hour inclusive of a one-minute stop at Bruges for the 71 miles (114.3 km) between Brussels and Ostend, and with an average speed of 75.3 mph (121.2 kph) between Brussels and Bruges nonstop they were the fastest steam-hauled trains in the world at that time, beating the current 74.6 mph (120.1 kph) average between Sparta and Portage of the 'Hiawatha' express of the Chicago, Milwaukee, St Paul & Pacific Railroad in the USA.

The return of the Atlantic as a first-line locomotive type in the 1930s was not confined to Belgium. Atlantics were built to work the 'Hiawatha' although a 4–6–4 joined them later on the heavier turns. In France a compound Atlantic dating from the 1906–07 period was rebuilt and streamlined in 1935 to work a fast business service between Paris and Lyons which had been provided previously by a Bugatti railcar. When patronage exceeded the railcar's capacity, the steam train was introduced, at first with three streamlined vehicles and later with a fourth. At that time the maximum permitted speed for a steam locomotive in France was 75 mph (120 kph) and the benefit of streamlining was seen mainly in reduced fuel consumption. In fact the timing for the journey had to be increased compared with the railcar, which was allowed to run at 87 mph (140 kph).

The Belgian Atlantic design for the Brussels–Ostend fliers of 1939 was a completely new engine. Two inside cylinders drove the leading coupled axle through short connecting rods only 8 feet 6 inches (2591 mm) long. The inside cylinder arrangement was supposed to give smoother running at high speeds. Steam generation was maximized by a water tube firebox. The driving wheel diameter was 6 feet 10.62 inches (2099 mm). Six locomotives were built, four with piston valves driven by outside Walschaerts valve gear and two with Dabeg and Caprotti poppet valve gear respectively.

Streamlining was less complete than in some locomotives of the period. The casing at the front end continued rearward along the top of the boiler to enclose the fittings. Separate plating extended from below the cab windows toward the front where it was swept upward to form smoke deflectors. An enclosure over the trailing wheels was lifted to clear the driving wheels completely but then dropped again in the vicinity of the cylinders, where it was pierced with large apertures for access to the valve gear. These apertures were permanently open, which not only spoiled the continuity of the streamlining, perhaps with some resultant drag, but did nothing to enhance the appearance of the locomotive. This part of the streamlining might better have been omitted completely.

An enclosure for the front buffer beam merged visually with the upper and side fairings and was carried downward almost to rail level. A large oval opening for the coupling also cleared the central headlight which was mandatory on Belgian steam locomotives. The sides of the spacious cab sloped sharply inward from below the side windows in order to conform with the streamlined contours.

These high-speed locomotives and trains created much public interest when they began running in May 1935. Crowds came to the station at Ghent to watch them flash through, and station staff held ropes along the platform edge to keep the spectators at a safe distance. Sometimes the formation was only three coaches, seating 12 first-class and 100 second-class passengers, but the maximum permitted load was five coaches. Some of the early trips were recorded by experienced observers. On a trial run with a five-coach train weighing 280 US tons/ 250 UK tons/254 tonnes the train reached a maximum speed of 102.5 mph (165 kph) on practically level track between Bruges and Ghent. In the course of the regular service one of the Atlantics reached 87 mph (140 kph) only 3.5 miles (5.6 km) out of Bruges on the run to Brussels and for the next ten miles (16.1 km) kept up a steady 90 mph (145 kph).

This special service was suspended on the outbreak of war in September 1939 but was resumed early in 1940. A high-speed service between Brussels and Liège using the streamlined Atlantics had been planned for the winter timetable of 1939 but was deferred. It was introduced on 15 March 1940 but doomed to be short-lived, for on 10 May Belgium was engulfed in the war.

Through the war years the Atlantics kept rolling, but on duties for which their large-diameter driving wheels were far from appropriate, such as heavy passenger trains on the Belgian section of the Brussels—Amsterdam route. After the war the essential reconstruction of track and equipment gave the opportunity for a new start in which electrification would play the major role, supported by diesel traction on lines remaining unelectrified. The Atlantics remained at work but never resumed their old duties although they were used for a time on a service of fast trains formed of lightweight rolling stock between Brussels and Tournai. They were withdrawn in 1961, deprived — first by the European turmoil and then by the reconstruction which followed — of the opportunity to show their full potential.

While much concerned with improving the speed of their express passenger trains, most railways in the second half of the 1930s were faced with the problem of providing local services that would retain traffic in the face of competition from private and public road transport and be economical to run. Belgium found a distinctive solution in its *trottinettes* or 'scooter trains.' A *trottinette* might consist of a veteran express locomotive or an old freight engine coupled to two coaches not much younger, but

renovated to provide acceptable accommodation. Instead of being broken up, this superannuated equipment was adapted to win back traffic on country and suburban routes subject to bus competition.

With their relatively powerful engines and light loads, the 'scooter' trains could accelerate smartly and run at quite high speeds. This meant that more stations and halts could be opened, giving convenient railway service to new areas, while overall journey times were still shorter than in the past. The light trains often ran at speeds around 60 mph (97 kph) between stops, which was much better than was achieved by most steam-hauled local trains at that time. Although the short formations meant limited seating capacity, the coaches were adapted internally to afford generous standing room, and as the majority of passengers by these services were making short station-to-station journeys the accommodation proved quite acceptable and the trains were a success.

The locomotives and rolling stock were nearing the end of their economic life but the experiment was too popular to be abandoned as withdrawals became necessary. By this time, however, the railways were purchasing diesel railcars for local services, and as the 'scooters' were taken out of service the railcars took over the routes, where they found a ready market which soon compensated for their rather higher initial cost.

Although the locomotives of Scandinavia all had to be capable of operating in subzero temperatures and, so far as Norway and Sweden were concerned, over mountainous conditions, they by no means developed a uniform appearance.

It would be difficult to look at any particular locomotive in Scandinavia and aver that it derived from Chapelon or Gresley, though one might look, for example, at a Dutch 2—8—0 freight of 1930 and suspect that there was something British-looking about it, or a Danish compound of 1907 and murmur 'France,' or even a Norwegian 4—8—0 four-cylinder compound and be distracted by a conversely Germanic-American flavor.

But if there was not a 'Scandinavian look,' there could be said to have been a 'Scandinavian style.' It was a style of performance brought about by the demands put upon locomotives in that part of the world by the conditions under which they worked and the nature of the tracks over which they operated. Topography dictated that the railways could not take heavy locomotives on many of their routes and axle-load restrictions were mostly below 17.6 US tons/15.7 UK tons/16 tonnes and sometimes even less than 12.1 US tons/10.8 UK tons/11 tonnes. There was, anyway, no great demand for express trains hauled by the high-powered locomotives to be found in nearby France and Germany.

Thus it was that in Denmark the native locomotive engineers were not required to produce designs for more than 4—6—0s and 2—8—0s to handle freight and passenger traffic over routes which were generally flat.

In 1922 Denmark introduced the three-cylinder simple arrangement of front drive with three separate valve gears. Outside valve gear had remained popular for main-line locomotives for considerably longer in Denmark than elsewhere and even in 1907 the Danish State Railway brought out a 4—4—2 which was a four-cylinder compound with

Above: Danish State Railways 4—4—0 No 8 makes a special run for enthusiasts from England in 1970.

**Right:** An American 'Austerity' 2–8–0 at Brussels in the early postwar years.

Above: The 4—4—0 wheel arrangement seems to encourage simplicity of external line, as exemplified in this Danish locomotive.

outside low-pressure cylinders and two multi-headed piston valves.

The 1922 three-cylinder simple was a 4—6—0 R2 class with coupled wheels of 6 feet 1.5 inches (1867 mm) diameter and a grate area of 28 square feet (2.60 sq m). Success with this design prompted the introduction two years later of a 2—8—0 M class, with a similar grate area and the same working pressure of 171 lb per square inch (12.0 kg/sq cm) but with wheels of 4 feet 7.25 inches (1403 mm) diameter. Next came a 2—6—4 tank three-cylinder single in 1925 with a lesser grate — 25.8 square feet (2.40 sq m) and 5 feet 8.5 inches (1740 mm) wheel diameter. This was the final home-inspired design and all three types used separate Walschaerts valve gears.

In 1936 Denmark bought 11 Swedish Pacifics which formed the basis of their principal express passenger type. A further 25 were built between 1943 and 1947 by Frichs of Denmark and the type continued in regular service until the 1960s. The Swedish Pacifics had been introduced in 1914 and had departed from previous design in Sweden by being compounds. Although the engines looked huge they, in fact, adhered to the 17.6 US ton/ 15.7 UK ton/16 tonne axle-load limit. The driving wheels were 6 feet 2 inches (1880 mm) in diameter and the grate 38.7 square feet (3.59 sq m). The outside cylinders of the four driving the intermediate coupled axle were inclined steeply.

A feature of the Swedish railway system was that it was not entirely state-owned and the fact that there was a degree of competition from private companies led to the introduction of a considerably larger number of locomotive types than elsewhere in Scandinavia. A number of these designs formed the basis for a useful export market, the chief exporters being Nydquist & Holm, who not only sent abroad locomotives built to Swedish requirements but also developed a good reputation for adaptations to suit the requirements of particular countries.

As part of this adaptive capability Nydquist & Holm produced some three-cylinder 2—8—2s for Iran in 1937. These were distinguished by their small-diameter wheels of 4 feet 5.12 inches (1349 mm) and large grates of 45 square feet (4.18 sq m).

A particularly interesting export order for the company came in 1942 from the Dutch government-in-exile in London. In all the government ordered 35 0—8—0s and 15 4—6—0s. The first orders were placed at a time when Holland had fallen into Nazi hands but deliveries did not begin until 1946, by which time the liberated country was desperately short of steam motive power.

Both the 0—8—0s and the 4—6—0s were three cylinder designs, each having the same diameter-stroke of 19.68 by 26 inches (500 by 600 mm). The 0—8—0 had 4-foot 5.12-inch (1349-mm) diameter wheels, a grate area of 32.3 square feet (3.0 sq m) and axle-load of 20.3 US tons/18.1 UK tons/18.5 tonnes. For the 4—6—0 the wheel diameter was 6 feet 2.37 inches (1890 mm), the grate area 35 square feet (3.25 sq m) and the axle-load 20 US tons/ 17.9 UK tons/18.3 tonnes. Unfortunately the coupled axle roller bearings of these otherwise very fine engines suffered severely from corrosion and consequently their working life was not very long.

A feature of Swedish locomotive design during the middle period of steam was that while inside cylinders were common, the outside return cranks used to work the links to the Walschaerts valves, together with high running plates above the coupled wheels of several types (notably 0—6—0s, 2—6—4Ts and 4—6—0s) gave a distinctive and slightly unbalanced appearance. Although compounding was then very rare, a particular exception is noted by the designer and prolific writer, E S Cox, in *World Steam in the Twentieth Century*. It was a 4—6—0 of 1914 with compound cylinders, 30 square feet (2.79 sq m) grate and an adhesive weight of 51.7 US tons/46.2 UK tons/47.1 tonnes. It was, says Cox, very typical in appearance with a totally enclosed windcutter cab, conical smokebox door, stovepipe chimney, combined dome and sandbox and a bogie with outside axleboxes and springs, a common feature on many classes.

The three-cylinder simple arrangement which Denmark introduced in 1922 was adopted by Sweden in 1930 for some 4—6—0s and it was also used in 1947 for Sweden's only 4—8—0 type.

If the Swedish 4—8—0 was a 'loner,' the type was extremely well used in neighboring Norway, increasing in popularity from 1910 until 1926. The early versions were either four-cylinder simples or compounds and — again with topography in mind — were restricted to axle weights of a mere 12.8 US tons/11.4 UK tons/11.6 tonnes, though later this was lifted to 15.3 US tons/13.7 UK tons/14 tonnes.

The largest Norwegian locomotive type ever built was also the last. It appeared in 1935 and was a 2—8—4 compound with an axle-load of 17.1 US tons 15.3 UK tons/15.6 tonnes and total weight of 108.5 US tons/96.5 UK tons/98.5 tonnes. The grate was a vast 53.8 square feet (5 sq m). The type, of which seven were built — five in Norway and two in Germany — was almost as curious as the 2—8—4s of 1928 produced in Austria and considerable ingenuity was used to make the locomotive as compact as possible and provide space for the big boiler. Only two prototypes of the design were produced, one being filled for a time with a booster. During World War II a considerable number of German class 52 2—10—0s were brought in by the occupying powers. These tough 'all-weather' engines were produced in profusion — a total of 6292 were built between 1942 and 1949 — and did stalwart work in their native Germany and in several occupied countries where they continued in service until the end of steam.

Finland in the 1930s was shaking off its image of being a country of wood-burning locomotives. The wood-burners were still about, with their bulbous

spark-arresting chimneys, but they were already being relegated to the slower services and their place taken on the expresses by 4–6–0s of a less picturesque but more efficient aspect. Although journeys were still made at an average speed not much above 40 mph (64 kph), even that called for considerably faster running than in the past.

The need for acceleration was felt as Finland began to attract more holiday visitors, some making their way to the lakes and others crossing the country to the Russian frontier. Parties visiting the Soviet Union from the United States often chose to travel via England and the weekly steamer from Hull to Helsinki, which called at Copenhagen en route, afforded them the opportunity for light relief before beginning their serious social studies. On such occasions the single sleeper for Leningrad would often need to be supplemented.

Travel in Finland was soothing. Strangely enough the shrill whistling of the locomotive at short intervals throughout the run was soporific rather than irritating. 'Peep! Peep!' piped the engine before every station and at all the countless level crossings, and the rhythm of the wheels seemed hardly to vary, for the main line from Helsinki to Viipuri and then on to the frontier station of Rajajoki is built along the level coastal plain. In the first few miles of the journey 'embankments' worthy of the name are non-existent and the rocky cuttings are shallow and short. Outside the carriage window streams past an almost

unbroken succession of straight-trunked trees, sometimes receding from the line a little to make room for a station and township but always present.

Second-class travel in those days cost the equivalent of about half an old penny per mile. The seats, with armrests, invited the traveller to sink back, but if he did so he missed much of the view because the windows were on the small side. But one noted that the native traveller was not much given to watching the scenery. Newspapers and magazines were sold by an attendant who patrolled the corridor, so the passenger relied largely on reading to occupy his mind. He also smoked, but instead of dropping his ash on the floor or on the knees of the man sitting opposite, he would lean across his neighbor with a murmured apology to drop it into one of the corner ashtrays.

The guard was an official more in evidence on Finnish trains in those days than in some countries. As the train slowed for a stop he looked into every compartment, announcing the name of the station, the length of stay, and the places for which it was necessary to change. When inspecting tickets he told every traveller his time of arrival, or where he must alight for a connecting train.

There was little first-class travel in Finland at that time. The only obvious difference between first and second classes was the fact that in the first-class passengers sat facing a blank wall instead of their opposite numbers. Third class passengers were admitted to all trains.

Steam locomotives in Holland as in Belgium long reflected early British design influence. The most numerous passenger class up to the 1930s was a four-cylinder simple 4—6—0 originally supplied by the Manchester firm of Beyer Peacock although construction was continued by continental firms. With its elegant chimney, its safety valve casing, and discreetly concealed auxiliaries it was a dignified machine with an imperturbable air that matched its competent but usually unhurried performance. Here there was none of the awesome aspect of the Flamme Pacifics over the border but a cool superiority commanding equal respect. A 4—6—4 tank engine version struck the same note. Some of the earlier locomotives from British companies enjoyed a long life. A 2—4—0 tank engine scrapped in September 1935 had been supplied to the Dutch Central Railway in 1863 by Neilson & Company of Glasgow and still carried a boiler that had been fitted in 1884. It had begun life as a tender engine but was rebuilt as a tank in the 1890s for work on branch lines and finished its career as shed pilot at Barneveld on the Nykerk-Ede branch of the old Central system. It was then the oldest locomotive in Holland, a distinction which passed on its retirement to a double-framed 0—6—0 freight engine which had been built by Beyer Peacock of Manchester in 1865.

At the end of the 1920s the Dutch railways were in the same position as railways almost everywhere – they needed more powerful locomotives for working heavier trains. Steel coaches were increasing the weights to be hauled, particularly on international services, and the earlier 4—6—0s were proving inadequate. The choice was between a Pacific with a 18-US-ton/16-UK-ton/16-tonne axle-load as in the preceding classes or a 4—6—0 with 20-US-ton/18-UK-ton/18-tonne axle-load. It was decided to adopt the ten-wheeler, a decision which made it necessary to strengthen a large number of bridges on the main lines. A design was produced in collaboration with the German firm of Henschel, and the first locomotives of the new class 3900 appeared at the end of 1929.

Deliveries of the remainder, bringing the total to 32, followed in April 1930. This was again a four-cylinder simple and had other technical characteristics similar to the earlier Beyer Peacock design such as drive on to the leading axle, and inside Walschaerts valve gear operating the valves of the inside cylinders direct and those of the outside cylinders through rocking shafts. Gone was the safety valve casing, but there was still a copper dome, and the chimney had a narrow copper cap to relieve the starkness of its stovepipe shape. In other respects the locomotives retained the classic simplicity of outline of their predecessors until trouble was experienced from steam from the short chimney interfering with the outlook from the cab, resulting in the second batch being fitted with smoke deflectors. Eventually the whole class was equipped in this way.

Tests with the first engines of the class were carried out on the Flushing-Tilburg section of the railway, hauling a train of 18 coaches over the distance of 74.5 miles (119.9 kph). In these conditions a speed of 68.4 mph (110.1 kph) was maintained and an output of 1600 hp was recorded. The new motive power was immediately distributed among the principal main-line depots for fast passenger duties. Among them were international trains to and from Germany, including the prewar 'Rheingold Express' between Amsterdam and the German frontier via Arnhem. They were also a familiar sight on express trains at the frontier stations of Oldenzaal and Venlo. In internal service they worked the route between Amsterdam and Maastricht; and from 1935, after strengthening of the bridges over the Ijssel, between Utrecht and Groningen.

Many of the 3900 class were sent to Germany during World War II. All returned eventually to Holland, but two of them were too badly damaged to be reinstated and were scrapped. Like many steam locomotives in the postwar years, their sphere of activity shrank with the spread of electrification and diesel traction. It was a time of miscellaneous duties and frequent transfers, ending in most of them being

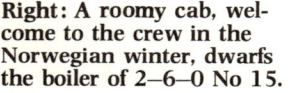

**Right: A roomy cab, welcome to the crew in the Norwegian winter, dwarfs the boiler of 2—6—0 No 15.**

concentrated at Nijmegen and Venlo. From 1951 the Venlo locomotives worked passenger turns between there and Eindhoven, including the 'Rheingold' and the lighter 'Rheinpfeil.' By that time the 'Rheingold' was taking the southerly route from the Hook of Holland via Rotterdam, Breda, Tilburg, Eindhoven and Venlo. They were also to be seen on less glamorous stopping services.

Nijmegen was the last major depot to house the 3900 class. They worked some military trains, particularly at weekends, also freight and coal traffic. Nijmegen depot was closed on 2 June 1957 and its locomotives sent to Roosendaal, where they lingered awaiting the end. The last of the class was withdrawn in December of that year.

The 3900 class was never as popular with the men as their predecessors, known affectionately as the 'Jumbos,' which were considered much easier to work. In particular, the 3900s were criticized for their appetite for coal, which threw a severe burden on the fireman when working heavy trains.

Freight traffic was also making more demands on locomotives as the 1930s dawned. The order for the 3900 class passenger engines was quickly followed by one for an equivalent freight locomotive, although this was a tank engine with the 4–8–4 wheel arrangement. Henschel delivered 12 in 1930 and

another 12 came from Schwartzkopff in 1931. They were known as class 6300. This was a welcome addition to the railways' motive power for goods traffic was still being worked to a large extent by six-coupled locomotives. A 2–8–0 version of the 'Jumbo' had been produced, but with two outside cylinders only, and it fell far short of the popularity of the passenger engines because of its bad riding. There were also some 2–8–2 tank engines but their small fuel capacity limited their usefulness. In many technical respects the 6300 engines were similar to class 3900. An unusual feature of the design was the absence of side tanks, all fuel supplies being carried behind the cab so that there was scarcely any effect on the adhesive weight while the locomotive was at work.

These were doughty engines. On a trial run from Tilburg to Roermond with a train of 20 passenger vehicles weighing about 780 (US) tons they reached 62 mph (100 kph) in places, and touched 37 mph (60 kph) with a 2016-US-ton/1800-UK-ton/1829-tonne freight train between Eindhoven and Utrecht. In exploits of this order their coal consumption was voracious, however, and the fireman's work was gruelling. The class was always employed in the south of the country and stayed there during most of World War II, but in 1944, when a number of

Above: A tender piled with wood and a spark-arresting chimney, as in this 2—8—0, were characteristic of Finnish steam power for many years. Right: A Dutch outside-framed 2—4—0 photographed in 1930 reflects early British influence. The maker's nameplate – Beyer Peacock & Co Ltd, Manchester – is on the splasher.

Dutch locomotives were taken to Germany by the retreating forces as a reprisal for the Dutch railway-men's strike, 11 of the 22 went with them. All but one were later retrieved but four were scrapped in 1947 as beyond repair.

Work for the engines diminished progressively after their return from Germany. They were first stationed at Venlo and Maastricht, but from May 1951 at Maastricht only. Here their duties included the incongruous task of hauling two-coach stopping passenger trains on the line to the Belgian frontier at Visé. Freight traffic was being handed over to diesels and by June 1957 the 6300s were working only two days a week on freight, with a daily stint of barely 87 miles (140 km). The first locomotive of the class, No 63001, made the last steam workings from Maastricht, the schedule running from 18 November 1957 until the depot closed on 6 January 1958.

Two locomotives were held back from scrapping. No 6305 was kept for a few years for testing bridges and relaid track, but not under steam, being propelled, with its coupling rods removed, by a diesel. It was later broken up. The story of No 6317 was happier. After withdrawal early in 1957 at Maastricht it was taken to Roosendaal and reconditioned for exhibition in the Railway Museum at Utrecht, where it was installed on 15 October 1959.

In the postwar years many locomotives were to be seen at work far from their home territories, among them Swedish locomotives in Holland. These were not on loan, however, but had been ordered from Swedish industry by the Dutch government-in-exile in London in 1842, anticipating the shortage of motive power that would be experienced when peace returned. There were two classes – a passenger 4—6—0, class 4000 and a freight 0—8—0 class 4700. Both were based on similar locomotives supplied to railways in Sweden by the builder, NOHAB, since the conditions in which the orders were placed precluded the preparation of new designs by the Dutch railway authorities. Both classes were three-cylinder simples with three sets of Walschaerts valve gear.

The 15 4—6—0s bore distinctive marks of their Swedish origin, such as a fully enclosed cab with rear wall, a common enclosure for the dome and sandbox, and roller bearings on all axles, including

Below: The ten-wheel arrangement was retained when Holland needed larger locomotives. No 3902 in this picture, taken in 1930, is one of the 3900 class 4—6—0s which appeared at the end of 1929. The design was produced in collaboration with Henschel in Germany.

152

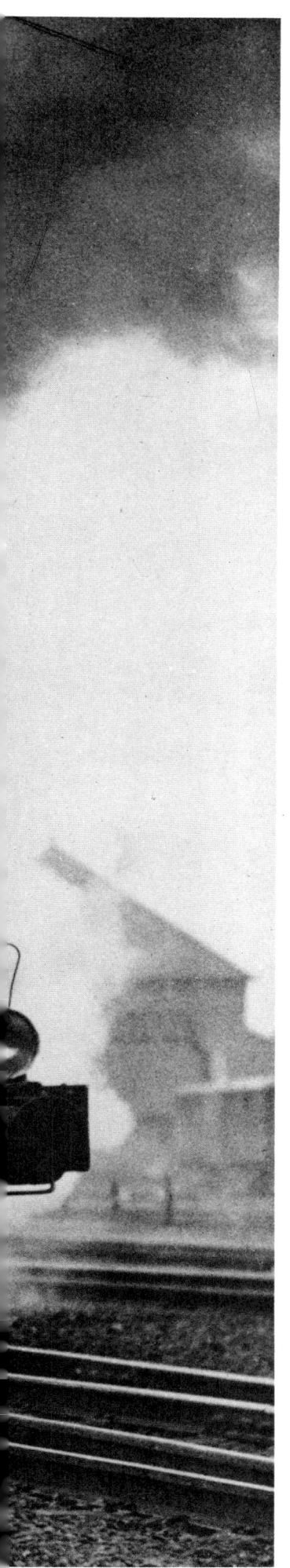

Above: A UK War Department 2–10–0 stands in Winscholen Station in 1947 with a train from Groningen.
Left: A 4–4–0 built for Holland by Sharp, Stewart in 1891 is returned from Germany at the beginning of 1946 much the worse for wear as a result of bombing.
Far left: The 'Great Eastern' look in inside-cylinder 4–6–0 No 3501 leaving Eindhoven with a northbound Netherlands Railways express in 1930.

the tender. Electric lighting included lamps for inspecting the motion. The front of the cab was of a 'wind-cutting' wedge shape and there was a self-cleaning smokebox, with an exceptionally small coned door. A door on the fireman's side of the cab led on to the running plate. With coupled wheels of 6 feet 2.5 inches (1892 mm) diameter, the maximum permitted speed was 74.5 mph (119.9 kph). Deliveries began in 1946. During their service in Holland the locomotives had their steel fireboxes changed for copper and a larger, flat smokebox door was fitted because it was found that the original pattern made tube cleaning very difficult.

The 4–6–0s were shedded first at Amsterdam and later at Rotterdam when through-workings between Amsterdam, Rotterdam and Belgium were restored. Later some of the engines were transferred to Eindhoven where they were used to some extent on goods traffic. After various other moves, all were concentrated at Amersfoort by the end of 1948.

The engines retained express workings between Amersfoort and Zwolle until that section was electrified on 7 January 1952. They were then virtually without suitable employment although barely six years old, but Amsterdam came to their rescue by allotting them a few express passenger turns on the line to Arnhem and Emmerich, the most important being the Holland–Italy express (Amsterdam–Rome), which was double-headed at times of peak traffic, and

the Amsterdam portion of the 'Rheingold.' These services, too, went over to electric traction from 5 January 1953. Withdrawals began of the members of the class which had not been rebuilt with copper fireboxes but those which had been so converted lingered on for a few more years. The remaining engines were finally withdrawn from service in the autumn of 1955.

The 0–8–0 freight locomotives of class 4700 had some typically Swedish features similar to those of class 4000, but also a powerful headlight and a cowcatcher. Both were removed, and the class was equipped with copper fireboxes and larger smokebox doors similarly to the 4–6–0s. Wheel diameter was 4 feet 5 inches (1346 mm) which nominally restricted the speed to 36 mph (58 kph) but the steady running of the engines enabled this to be raised to 43.5 mph (70 kph).

All the engines began their service at Amersfoort, where they also worked a few passenger turns. They later moved to Eindhoven and Heerlen where they worked on coal trains from the collieries to the Susteren marshalling yard. Sometimes the coal trains were very heavy and at times Heerlen had to provide a banking locomotive for the climb from Haanrade to Schaesberg. At the end of 1957 two engines of this class were the last in steam on the Netherlands Railways. With their withdrawal the steam era in Holland finally ended.

# 8. Austria and Eastern Europe

The country of Viennese waltzes, the Radetzky March and the Congress of 1815 was also the country of the Semmering Trials, Gölsdorf locomotives and the Giesl ejector. Karl Gölsdorf, who joined the Imperial State Railways of Austria–Hungary in 1891, made his name synonymous with compounding and long coupled wheelbases. He died in 1916, but his work had already strongly influenced the surrounding countries where lines traversed mountainous regions. Gölsdorf designed his locomotives with coupling rods and axlebox guides which allowed sideplay in certain coupled axles, so that high adhesion was obtained without rigidity, and locomotives with four-, five- or even six-coupled axles could operate on steeply graded routes with severe curvature which previously had required some form of articulated locomotive.

Gölsdorf first adopted a flexible coupled wheelbase in the class 170 2–10–0 introduced in 1897 for passenger service on mountain routes. In replacing the 0–6–0s which had been used up to then on the Arlberg route it was an immediate success, doubling the loads hauled. The same type was adopted by the Sudbahn (privately owned until 1924) for its line over the Brenner Pass. Some 800 locomotives were built to this design for Austria and neighboring countries, construction continuing until 1919, and they were to be seen on freight service over 40 years after they were introduced. A superheated version was classified 270.

The first full application of Gölsdorf's principles came in his class 180 0–10–0 of 1900. Here the first, third and fifth axles had a sideplay of 0.24 inches (6.1 mm) in each direction. The second and fourth axles were fixed, the latter being the driving axle. To avoid having a very heavy connecting rod, the piston rod was extended and the crosshead worked in slidebars fixed well in the rear of the cylinders in front of the second coupled axle. Experience showed that the sideplay of the rear coupled axle caused bad riding on straight track or curves of large radius and in later years this axle was fixed. No 1 of class 180 is preserved in the Technical Museum in Vienna.

At the turn of the century new rail routes were being built in the mountainous regions of Austria to improve north–south communications for internal and international traffic. In 1906 Gölsdorf introduced a 2–10–0 four-cylinder compound for these lines. This design, class 280, was to replace the class 170s on the heaviest express duties and for many years it remained the standard main-line passenger design on all severely graded routes of the State Railways. It was ready in time for the opening of the Tauernbahn in 1909. The Tauernbahn was a north–south link which in conjunction with other new construction further south significantly reduced the

Left: A class 33 4–8–0 of the ÖBB (Österreichische Bundesbahnen) heads a tourist train in Western Carinthia in the summer of 1957.

Above: Ten-coupled loco-
motives were widely used
on steeply graded main
lines in Austria. No 58.750,
a 2—10—0, has brought a
freight train to Oeblarn,
between Selzthal and
Bischofshofen, in 1957,
toward the end of its
working life.

distance by rail between Southern Germany. Salzburg and the port of Trieste. It extended from Schwar-
zach St Veit to Spittal-Millstattersee, a distance of
49.7 miles (80 km) and crossed the intervening
mountain range in the Tauern Tunnel, 5 miles
1550 yards (9464 m) long. Maximum gradient was
1-in-35.7, and 55 percent of the route was at this
inclination.

An impressive array of expresses crossed the
Tauern range by this route. There were four through-
trains daily between Salzburg and Trieste up to the
outbreak of World War I, two with restaurant cars
throughout, and a further connection with only one
change. One of the trains included an American-
style Pullman Car built in Austria under an arrangement with Canadian Pacific, which had begun direct
sailings between Canada and Trieste. From Spittal the
trains followed an existing line to Villach and there
joined further new sections which pierced the Kara-
wanken Range in a tunnel 4 miles 1682 yards
(7975 m) long and also provided a cut-off to Trieste
from Klagenfurt for trains from Vienna as well as for
through-services via Linz from the spas of Bohemia
(Czechoslovakia), Prague, Dresden and Berlin.

In the days before air transport, such routes provided lucrative traffic, much of its first class, and

received special attention from motive power authorities. Gölsdorf followed his 2—10—0s with a 2—12—0
designed specifically for the Tauernbahn. This was
another four-cylinder compound with his characteristic features. Drive was on the third coupled axle
and the driving wheels were flangeless. Sideplay was
allowed for the second, fifth and sixth coupled axles.
The locomotive, No 100.01, might have been the
forerunner of a whole class of 2—12—0s but at the
time it was introduced much new construction of
locomotives for general service was in hand and
further work on this specialized design had to be
deferred. Three years after it appeared, Austria was
involved in World War I and so No 100.01 remained
unique. By 1914 it had amply demonstrated that the
12-coupled wheelbase caused no abnormal wear of
the coupled wheels and it seems that the authorities
were satisfied — a memorandum from the Transport
Ministry to the State Railways management dated 9
September 1914 noted that in order to improve the
capacity of the line between Assling (Jesenice) and
Trieste it was proposed to authorize nine more class
100 locomotives, which could become a future
standard for heavy express, general passenger and
freight traffic on this line. The plans were shelved
during the war and were not revived afterwards

**Above left: One of the ubiquitous Class 52s, No 52.1442, on shed at Vienna East.**
**Above: A veteran Hungarian 0—6—0 is still at work at Eger in 1975.**
**Above right: Front-end detail of a class 52 at Vienna East shed.**
**Left: Hungarian local steam in a hurry.**

because in 1920 the decision was taken to electrify the Tauernbahn.

No 100.01 spent its working life of some 15 years on the Tauern section, but as the schedules were still based on the capacity of the 2—10—0s it was rarely extended unless lost time had to be recovered. After a spell out of traffic for display at the Munich Transport Exhibition in 1925 it was returned to service equipped with a Dabeg feedwater heater, but was withdrawn in 1928 and broken up. It was not without its influence on future locomotive design, however, for it was the basis of the Wurtemburg State Railway 2—12—0s of 1917 (later Deutsche Reichsbahn class 59) and by a turn of events then unforeseen these engines were sent to work in Austria during World War II. They had coupled wheels of 4 feet 5.12 inches (1349 mm) diameter compared with 4 feet 8.12 inches (1425 mm) in class 100 and were used extensively for heavy freight as well as passenger traffic. To improve tender-first running the sixth coupled axle was given more sideplay than in class 100 but was controlled by coil springs which came into action after a deflection of 1.1 inch (28 mm) and thereafter exerted a progressively increasing restoring force up to the maximum deflection of 1.75 inches (44 mm). This was to relieve the forces on the fifth axle, which was fixed. The locomotives that remained in Austria after the war were reclassified OBB class 659. In their last days in Austria they worked on heavy freight duties on the Semmering line, including banking, and also from Villach to Tarvis and Jesenice.

Only a small segment of Gölsdorf's work can be considered here, but it must be added that his four-coupled and six-coupled classes included a 2—6—4 tender engine for passenger traffic and an Atlantic. The 2—6—4s were built first in 1908 as saturated steam engines (class 210) and later with superheaters (class 310). Their high running plates fully exposed their large driving wheels of 6 feet 10.75 inches (2102 mm) diameter giving them a speed capability which enabled them to work side by side with more modern classes in express passenger duties until the

late 1930s. By 1919, however, it was evident that there would not be work for the whole series in Austria and the last ten to be built were sold abroad. Seven went to the Prussian State Railways and three to the Polish State Railways. By 1922 the seven in Prussia were surplus to requirements and joined the others in Poland, with the curious sequel that after the German occupation of Poland in World War II all ten were sent back to Austria and worked there for the first time during the war years.

Gölsdorf's Atlantic (class 108) of 1901 is said to have been inspired by his admiration for British locomotives seen during a visit in 1899. He was impressed by the blend of utility and elegance achieved by British designers and sought a similar effect. How well he succeeded could be seen as late as 1929 when the last three of class 108 were still working the Vienna—Nice—Cannes Express out of Vienna as far as Gloggnitz, where the stiffest part of the climb over the Semmering begins. The Atlantics had been designed specifically for the Vienna—Prague main line, where they could take 258-US-ton/230-UK-ton/234-tonne trains up long, winding gradients at 46 mph (74 kph). Their 7-foot (2134-mm) diameter wheels gave them a good turn of speed on the easier stretches. Until 1930 the maximum permitted service speed in Austria was 62.1 mph (100 kph) but on a test run one of the Atlantics attained 89.5 mph (144 kph).

In the years after World War I Gölsdorf's successors were faced by the then-widespread demand for locomotives to work heavier trains at higher speeds. During the war the Sudbahn had introduced two powerful 4—8—4 locomotives for working between Trieste and Ljubljana and they were so successful that the State Railways adopted the design almost unchanged for the class 113 4—8—4s of 1923, apart from substituting poppet valves for piston valves. Forty were built in four years for express traffic on the Westbahn and Sudbahn routes under the supervision of J Rihosek, and they remained the most numerous class on the services from Vienna to Yugoslavia and Italy via the Semmering until diesels were introduced, pending electrification, after World

Above: A Czech 2–6–2 of the interwar years at Pilsen.
Left: Class 433 2–8–2T No 019 of the Czechoslovak Railways (CSD) wanders through the woods at Skalice with forestry products. This class was still at work in 1977 although being replaced by diesels.
Below left: The 4–8–0s of class 424 first appeared in 1924 and lasted to the end of steam. No 424.339 arrives at Budapest West with a push-and-pull train.

War II. Between 1955 and 1957 they were given a new lease on life by being equipped with Giesl ejectors and a higher superheat. Thus fortified, they coped single-handed with trains of 17 coaches weighing 840 US tons/750 UK tons/762 tonnes on gradients of 1-in-125. In these days of electric locomotives gliding smoothly over the Semmering, it requires some imagination to recreate the sight and sound of one of Rihosek's 4–8–4s thumping its way through the mountains aided by two of the same engineer's 2–10–2 tank engines, for here the line climbs from the west at nearly 1-in-35 to the summit.

In the years immediately after World War I Austria energetically tackled the task of strengthening the permanent way and structures on the principal routes within its new and contracted frontiers so that axle-loads could be increased from 14.5 to 16 Mp. Locomotive designers were therefore given more latitude in creating powerful types and steam development reached its peak with the construction under Rihosek's successor, A Lehner, of two prototype 2-8-4 express locomotives. The immediate purpose was to supersede ten-coupled types on the Westbahn and eliminate double heading, while the journey times of heavy trains would be cut by the ability to haul them over the steeply graded sections at 37.2 mph (60 kph). Maximum speed of the new design was to be 75 mph (120 kph) and both prototypes had 6-foot 2.75-inch (1.89-m) coupled wheels. Both were simple-expansion engines, one with two and the other with three cylinders.

The first prototype completed was the two-cylinder design. On test it attained 97 mph (156 kph) and proved so satisfactory in all respects that six more were ordered, followed by a further six in 1932. These locomotives formed class 214. The three-cylinder prototype, which appeared later and was less favorable in several respects including fuel consumption, was designated class 114 and no more were built.

At first the class 214 locomotives were put into service on the Westbahn between Vienna and Salzburg or Passau and often improved on their rated performance of working 560-US-ton/500-UK-ton/508-tonne trains over 1-in-100 gradients at 37 mph (60 kph). After World War II electrification of the Westbahn progressively reduced their territory and

when the work was completed on 19 December 1952 the class became redundant. A few were transferred to express duties on the Sudbahn where they worked for a number of years, but the fixed pivot of the trailing bogie in No 2 to No 13 of the class, with no sideplay, was a disadvantage on the 206.7-yard (189-m) radius curves of the Semmering section. After electrification of the Sudbahn lines in Lower Austria on 29 September 1956 withdrawals began. The same design had a longer working life in the USSR however, where 79 similar locomotives were built under license from 1936 onward and were still at work in the 1970s.

The search for steam in its final years made widely familiar the names of many lines which were little known outside their immediate neighborhood. Among them was the 'iron-ore railway' in Austria on the eastern slopes of the Tauern range, which were a source of valuable ore. Rail communication reached the mining center of Vordernberg when a line was opened from Leoben in 1872. At the end of the 1880s the mining company was granted a concession to build a standard-gauge line from Eisenerz, on the other side of the mountain, to Vordernberg, via the Präbichl Pass. It was opened to freight traffic in September 1891 and to passengers in June 1892. The line rises 1680 feet (512 m) from Eisenerz to Präbichl in a distance of 7.5 miles (12.1 km) and then falls through 1430 feet (436 m) in the next 5 miles (8 km) to Vordernberg. With gradients steeper than 1-in-14, the line was worked on the Abt rack system over 9 miles (14.5 km) of its length. In the course of time the loading point for ore was moved from Eisenerz to Erzberg, from where the maximum gradient to the summit at Präbichl was approximately 1-in-18 . Only empty trains then had to be worked over the steeper sections.

The first motive power for the line was a class of 0–6–2 tanks 18 of which were delivered between 1890 and 1908, and nine were still at work in 1975. They handled all freight and passenger traffic on the line until joined in 1912 by Karl Gölsdorf's 0–12–0 tanks of class 269 (later classified 197).

These two classes lasted until the end of steam, and the sight and sounds of steam trains on the 'Iron Mountain' have been preserved for posterity in countless photographs and tape recordings. Often trains were worked by two locomotives, one of each class, one at the head and the other in the rear.

In Gölsdorf's 0–12–0s the coupled axles were in two groups of three, with an interval of 7 feet 6 inches (2286 mm) between the third and fourth to allow room for the two cogwheels of the rack system. The outside cylinders drove the fourth coupled axle, and two steeply inclined inside cylinders drove the rear cogwheel axle. The bearings for the two coupled cogwheel axles were in a subframe supported by the third and fourth adhesion axles.

The first of the 0–12–0s was not withdrawn until 1975, by which time the tonnage of ore moved over the rack section was declining. From 1923 railbuses took over most of the passenger workings, although one steam-hauled passenger train continued to run on working days between Vordernberg and Eisenerz. But visitors came in large numbers to see this last refuge of Austrian steam, and in 1970 a sleeping car worked over the line for the first time, conveying a party of enthusiasts from Germany. The Iron Mountain Railway shared with the Indonesian State Railways the distinction of being the last lines in the world to operate nonarticulated 12-coupled steam locomotives.

It had been proposed to modernize the Erzberg motive power in 1938, and A Lehner produced a 2–12–2 design of which two examples were built, the first appearing in 1941. Little was done with them during the war apart from ironing out a few weaknesses which showed themselves in service. After the war it was intended to strengthen the rack so that their full tractive effort could be utilized. There was more urgent work to be done, however, and a general shortage of materials, so that the strengthening was not put in hand and the 2–12–2s only found limited use. One was preserved in the 1960s but the other was scrapped. If they had been able to exert themselves to the full, they would have been the most powerful rack locomotives in the world.

Under Gölsdorf and his successors Austrian locomotive design was innovative in many respects and this spirit was seen at work to the end in the development of the Giesl ejector to improve the blast and increase the efficiency of the steam locomotive. To eyes unaccustomed to such things, the large spark arresters characteristic of Austrian freight locomotive chimneys until the early 1920s gave an impression of obsolescence which was totally undeserved. These rather unsightly fitments were necessary because of the lignite mixture fuel being burned at that period.

Above: First locomotives of the post-1945 standard programs in Czechoslovakia were the express passenger 4—8—2s of class 498.0. No 498.030 in blue livery leaves Tabor with the 13.08 Ceske Budejovice–Prague stopping train in June 1969. Above left: From 1952 onward over 500 2—10—0s of class 556.0 were built for heavy freight. No 556.0166 nears Bilovice with a southbound freight on the Ceska Trebova–Brno main line on 10 June 1969. Left: Class 434.2 locomotives (2—8—0) were among the standard Czech designs of the 1920s. No 434.2129 leaves Nezamyslice with a goods train for Olomouc on 9 June 1969.

Frontier changes in Europe after World War I were reflected in the locomotive stock of the countries affected. Hungary lost its mountainous regions, and locomotives built to work in those surroundings were often dispersed among the newly created states which inherited them. Some of the interwar express 4—6—0s of class 327 returned to Hungary in 1942, however, and their tall chimneys, massive boiler mountings, and 6-foot (1829-mm) diameter driving wheels, fully exposed by the high running plate except for the top segment of the rear pair, were still to be seen at the head of secondary passenger trains in the 1970s. Often behind the sand dome there would be the horizontal drum of the Brotan boiler, a feature much used in Hungary. In this construction the usual form of firebox was replaced by an assembly of tubes communicating at one end with the normal boiler and at the other with the drum, which acted as a steam collector and was itself linked with the boiler through two or more tubes. Still more numerous on secondary trains were the standard 2—6—2 tender engines of class 324 which were built in large numbers up to the early 1920s.

Hungary had its Atlantics, class 203, which gave good service until the late 1940s, and its Pacifics, class 301, built in 1911–13 for the mountainous line in Transylvania. Some of these went to Rumania in 1919. A few lingered in Hungary but by the middle 1960s were moribund. At one time Hungary had the largest fleet of Mallet articulated-tender engines in Europe and introduced its most powerful design, the 2—6—6—0 of class 601 in 1914, but all were dispersed after 1919, there being no further work for them in their homeland.

The large 4—8—0s of class 424 came out first in 1924. They increased rapidly in numbers, particularly during World War II, and construction continued afterwards. Many were supplied to Yugoslavia, Czechoslovakia and the USSR. Some of the USSR engines returned later to Hungary where they became the most widely used class until the end of steam. An impressive express 4—6—4 was built after the war but the class only numbered two engines and there was little demand for them in the timetables then being operated; 4—8—0s were more suitable for schedules calling for only modest maximum speeds

161

Left: Austrian State Railways 2-8-2 tank No 93309 on a branch-line service close to the Czech border.
Far right: In Austria steam has lingered on especially in the form of the ex-German 'Kreigslok' 2-10-0, a wartime engine. This picture showing one of the class fitted with a modern Giesl ejector multiple blastpipe chimney and short smoke deflectors was taken on Vienna East shed in 1968.
Right: PKP class PL 47 2-8-2 waits to leave Torun with a local train formed of double-deck stock.

Below: A Polish goods yard. A PKP class Ty23 2-10-0 shunts a train of empties over a hump at Pyskowice.

and involving frequent stops.

The creation of Czechoslovakia in 1918 resulted in a railway system equipped with a varied assortment of locomotives from different sources, counting nearly 200 different types in all. Works in Prague (CKD) and Pilsen (Skoda) took part in a standardization program based at first on Austrian practice but moving gradually towards a distinctive national locomotive identity. In World War II these factories had to build German *Kriegslokomotiven*. Most of those from Skoda remained in Czechoslovakia after the war as class 555.3. They were still to be seen at work around Breclav in 1977.

In the immediate postwar years Czechoslovakian builders produced over 500 2–10–0s based on the prewar 534.0 class and classified 534.03. Standardization began again with an express passenger 4–8–2 produced in 1946 and classified 498.0. It has much in common with the 486.0 class, a three-cylinder design built between 1934 and 1938. The same wheel arrangement was used for the mixed-traffic class 475.1 which followed but this two-cylinder series introduced more recent practice such

as a taper boiler, combustion chamber and thermic siphon, and roller bearings throughout. In a short series with smaller wheels and higher boiler pressure which followed there was a reversion to three cylinders but this time with compound working, surprisingly in view of the fact that earlier Czech three-cylinder compounds had all been converted to simples.

A further development from the prewar 486.0 class was a new express passenger 4–8–2 which came out in 1954. This was Czechoslovakia's final contribution to the steam express passenger engine; it was again a three-cylinder simple design but it incorporated many refinements and had an impressive appearance.

The most numerous class of locomotives still operating in the 1970s were the class 556.0 freight 2–10–0s, of which over 500 were built between 1952 and 1957. Steam fanciers who visited Czechoslovakia in the final years still speak of the staccato crackle of their double-Kylchap exhaust, perhaps the most characteristic steam sound in Czechoslovakia. These engines were known to work 560-US-ton/500-UK-ton/508-tonne trains single-handed and coped with 336 US tons/300 UK tons/305 tonnes even on steeply graded routes, although double-heading was common and sometimes heavy freights could be seen being urged westward out of Puchov by three, or sometimes four engines of the class.

A highly characteristic Czech locomotive class was the 4–8–4 passenger tank manufactured from 1951 onward. The first 38 were similar to a solitary engine of that wheel arrangement built in 1935 in that coal and water supplies were carried behind the cab. In later builds from 1955 onward some of the water was carried in small side tanks. These were well for-

Far left: Class 477.0 was the larger of two 4–8–4 tank engine classes of post-1945 construction. No 477.036 approaches Neza-myslice with the 13.55 Brno–Prerov train on 9 June 1969.
Far left below: One of the 4–8–0s built in Hungary for the Yugoslav railways follows a winding track through the mountains with a train of mixed freight and passenger stock. On the left is the 2ft 6in narrow gauge.
Below left: A Yugoslav Pacific at Belgrade in 1969 carries the national flag on its smoke deflectors.
Left: A 2–10–2T of the Bulgarian State Railways (narrow-gauge section) on a Cerven/Breg to Orjahavo train.

ward of the cab and the intervening space was filled by a false tank to give continuity of line. In later years the original engines were equipped with similar tanks but the false tank was omitted, leaving the former isolated and conspicuous. If there was discontinuity here, however, amends were made by the neat continuous enclosure of the boiler mountings, giving the locomotives an uninterrupted 'skyline.' The modified engines and those built later constituted class 477.0.

Yugoslavia was another complex political and geographical creation with inherited motive power. At first, construction of classes originating in Serbia was continued but in 1930 three designs specific to the new Yugoslav requirements were delivered. They were a Pacific for express service, a mixed traffic 2–8–2 and a standard freight 2–10–0. In the later 1930s a number of 2–4–2 tanks of Hungarian design were acquired, some of which were built in Yugoslavia. World War II brought Deutsche Reichsbahn 2–10–0s of class 52 into the country, some of which were retained afterward and joined by over 200 more. American standard

Top left: Bulgarian Monster:
One of Europe's most
powerful tank locomotives
ran over the BDZ (Bulga-
rian State Railways) metals.
Used to head heavy freights
up the grades out of Sofia
to Pernick, these grand
monsters were gone from
active service by 1966.
Today some are still in
evidence dumped at a loco
graveyard to Valkerel near
Sofia.

Top center: Hungary still
uses steam today but even
though it is kept in first-
class condition, it is dying
fast. One of the most
ubiquitous classes (still in
use) is the 424 class 4–8–0
used, as the British class 5
was, on almost any type of
train. No 424.339 was at
Budapest West in 1975
ready to work a push-and-
pull suburban train.

Top right: Czech express:
CSD class 475 4–8–2 No
475.1125 threads the
Svitava Valley near Bilovice
with a Semlly-to-Brno fast.
Right: A German built
(Prussian P8) 4–6–0 heads
a northbound local through
the Fin Gorge, Rumania.

Center: A 2–10–0 of the Hellenic State Railways 'belches black smoke' (perhaps the very 'vast, unkempt 2–10–0' of the traveller's tale in this chapter).
Below: The 'Orient Express,' looking rather less than romantic at the end of its lengthy journey, creaks to a halt near the steam shed before the change to electric traction for the last stage of the run to Istanbul.

Top right: Trains passing at Plovdin station in Bulgaria are both headed by 2–10–0 locomotives with a distinctive type of smoke deflector perched on top of the smokebox.
Bottom right: A train from the meter-gauge section of the Greek railways west of Athens arrives in Athens station behind an American-built 2–8–2 in 1964.

Left: Bulgarian State Railways double-headed freight train close to Sofia.
Below: A German abroad. An ex-German State Railways *Kriegslok* 2–10–0 with a passenger train in southern Turkey in 1977.

types made up immediate postwar motive power shortages, and Yugoslavia took the largest number of the 'Liberation' class 2–8–0s built in Great Britain for countries hard hit by wartime destruction or depletion of motive power.

The postwar locomotives in Yugoslavia with the most interesting history were the 4–8–0s of the Hungarian 424 class, some of which remained in Yugoslavia after the war. In 1947–48 a further 49 were delivered from Hungary, but as Hungary was now under the aegis of Josef Stalin and as the political 'coldness' developed between the USSR and Yugoslavia, the supply dried up. By 1955, however, there was a change of heart in high places and ten more of these engines were delivered.

Visitors to Orahovia, some 31 miles (50 km) north of Slavonski Brod, can see a diminutive 0–12–0 tank engine that worked for over 25 years on a meter-gauge mineral railway in Yugoslavia and is now preserved. The locomotive was built by Krauss Maffei in 1939 for the S H Gutmann Company in Belsice. This concern had its own railway to serve a quarry. In a distance of 2.75 miles (4.43 km) the line climbed 738 feet (225 m), equivalent to an average gradient of 1-in-20, and much of it was on curvature of 98 feet 5 inches (30 m) radius. For a quarter of the distance the gradient was between 1-in-13.3 and 1-in-12.5. Trains of empty wagons weighing 4032 lb (1829 kg) each had to be hauled up the hill to a quarry at the top, returning to the valley with a payload of 157 US tons/140 UK tons/142 tonnes. These conditions were more severe than faced by any rack locomotive of similar wheel arrangement.

Wheel diameter was as small as practicable at 2 feet 3.5 inches (698 mm), and with a minimum spacing of 2 feet 6.37 inches (771 mm) between coupled axles the total wheelbase was 13 feet 7 inches (4.14 m). Overall length of the locomotive was 27 feet 1 inch (8.26 m). The leading and trailing pairs of coupled axis were carried in pivoted subframes which also allowed some sideways displacement of individual axles, and the coupling rods had ball-and-socket joints for the same purpose. Outside cylinders drove the third coupled axle which, with the fourth axle, had bearings in the main frames. In the absence of trailing wheels, bunker capacity was limited and the locomotive usually operated coupled to a wagon carrying a reserve fuel supply.

The mountainous Balkans provided a natural home for the long coupled wheelbase. Bulgaria had two 12-coupled classes – an 0–12–0T and a 2–12–4T – both for freight. The 0–12–0 had been ordered on the eve of World War I but could not be delivered until 1922. It was designed for coal traffic on the section of 21 miles (33.8 km) between Sofia and the mining center of Pernik, where an average gradient of 1-in-38 extends for 6.8 miles (10.9 km) and there is a curvature of 902 feet (275 m) radius. There were ten engines in the class, two-cylinder compounds with a low-pressure cylinder no less than 15.75 cubic feet (445 liters) in volume, which was the biggest in Europe. At first the locomotives were not superheated, but superheaters were fitted later and the piston valves replaced with Lentz poppet valves. The first of the class were not withdrawn until 1973. Originally class 40, the locomotives became class 47 after superheating and conversion to poppet-valve gear.

The second 12-coupler for Bulgaria was a 2–12–4T intended primarily for the Pernik–Sofia coal traffic

as a successor to the 0–12–0s. (The latter had proved so satisfactory, particularly since being superheated, that they continued working side by side with the larger engines after deliveries began in 1931.) The first batch of 2–12–4s came from a Polish builder who supplied 14 in all. These were two-cylinder simples with superheaters. During World War I more locomotives of the same type were needed and were built in Germany by Schwartzkopff, but these final eight units of the class were three-cylinder machines with divided drive, the outside cylinders driving the third axle as before but the inside cylinder drove the second axle. The fuel capacity of these locomotives was greater than that of many tender engines and in their later years they were moved to longer-distance runs on the new west–east direct line from Sofia through Karlovo to Kazanlik and on to the Black Sea at Burgas. Here they worked trains of up to 1030 US tons/920 UK tons/935 tonnes over the 1-in-62.5 gradients which face trains crossing the watershed between Sofia and Kazanlik in either direction. As diesel and electric traction in Bulgaria was extended, withdrawals of the 2-12-4s began and they had gone by 1973.

Development in locomotives of more conventional wheel arrangements in Bulgaria took a new turn early in the 1930s when the maximum permitted axle-load was increased from 16 to 20 US tons. German design influence was strong, and classes with eight- or ten-coupled wheels were often favored both for passenger and freight traffic. At first two-cylinder types predominated but in 1935 three-cylinder propulsion was chosen for some new 2–8–2s. Early in World War II a similar design with a leading bogie was produced (4–8–2) together with a generally similar 4–10–0 for mixed traffic. By this time the latter were the only locomotives in the world with that wheel arrangement.

The traveller across Europe by one of the Orient Express services in the 1930s could enjoy an interesting panorama of steam motive power in some of the less visited countries. One who used the through coaches of the Arlberg-Orient Express recorded his impressions in lively style. He arrived at Athens by sea from Egypt on his way home to England and on going to the station was surprised to find that the Hellenic State Railways still followed the practice in 1939 of locking passengers in the waiting room until their train was at the platform. He was released on the arrival of nine coaches for various destinations, the rear two being resplendent blue Wagons-Lits cars labelled for Paris, one by the Simplon-Orient service and the other by the Arlberg-Orient. In due course 'a vast, unkempt 2–10–0 appeared, belching black smoke.' No doubt this was one of the 40 locomotives of Austrian parentage ordered in the 1920s which remained the principal Greek main-line class for two decades, supplemented later by some more engines of the same wheel arrangement loaned to Greece by Austria.

The journey to Salonika was exciting for its scenery rather than for speed, the train groaning its way round fearsome hairpin bends and threading breathtaking gorges and chasms; then smoother running, followed by reversal in Salonika and departure after a wait of half-an-hour behind 'another vast and sluggish 2–10–0' bound for the Yugoslav frontier.

The Yugoslav 2–6–2 which took over at the frontier station of Devedelija was viewed more ap-

Above: Pt47 class 2–8–2 No Pt47–13 looms over the evening rush-hour scene at Lublin station. This class was a postwar development of class Pt31, which was based on a German design.
Right: Polish State Railways 4–6–0 of class OK22, a Polish development of the Prussian P8. The locomotive is at Choszczno shed.

Below: Turkish State Railways 2–8–0 – one of the LMS Stanier-design locomotives supplied to the Middle East during World War II and still at work in 1979.
Far right: Arrival of the Mail. The daily Victoria Falls-to-Bulwayo passenger train – the mail, at Bulawayo in 1973. The engine is a 4–6–4+4–6–4 Garratt. This was an overnight train with full dining and sleeping-car facilities.

Right: South African Railways GMA class Garratt with a freight train taking water before climbing over the Lootsberg Pass.
Center right: South African Railways 4–8–2 locomotive at Port Elizabeth.

provingly as 'shapely and sprightly-looking' but this did not save it from running short of breath from time to time. A glance at the tender supplied the reason: 'the coal would not have been accepted at a slag heap in Lancashire.' Engines were changed (another 2–6–2) at Skolpje and the journey continued to Nis where a portion from Istanbul was attached. The 2–6–2, probably inherited from the Serbian Railways or one of the batch of 120 built in 1922–23, was now replaced by 'a rousing great Pacific of obvious German parentage.' Forty two-cylinder Pacifics were built for Yugoslavia by Schwartzkopff and were mainly used in the flatter territory between Nis and Beograd (Belgrade).

The Pacific steamed away from Nis with a train now composed entirely of Wagons-Lits stock, half Arlberg-Orient and half Simplon-Orient. From Beograd, where there was much splitting up and shunting in the night hours, the two services took different routes and the Arlberg coaches were taken on to the Hungarian frontier by 'a Yugoslav 4–6–0 of startling appearance, as hung-about with gadgets as a wartime soldier.' It was exchanged for 'an equally gaunt Hungarian sister, also a 4–6–0 and equally hideous with excrescences' (one of which was probably the horizontal drum of the Brotan boiler). And so to Budapest and more shunting, the Arlberg-Orient coaches from Bucharest being attached during various interesting early-morning maneuvers. The despised Hungarian 4–6–0 rolled away to its depot and an electric locomotive backed on to the train. The perspicacious recorder of this epic journey thought he detected a difficulty in cornering as the train rolled on to Hegyeshalom across the Great Hungarian Plain, ceremonially saluted at its passage through every station by the station staff lined up on the platform. He suggested that the problem might be the centrifugal effect of 'the immense revolving armature inside.' He may have been right, for not only would there have been the single massive traction motor for the side-rod drive but also the machine which converted the 50Hz single-phase supply in the contact wire into three-phase current. Electric locomotives were more impressive in the days before almost everything which revolves was tucked away in the bogies or hung below the underframe.

Steam resumed control at the Austrian frontier and the journey continued behind a 2–6–2 'of modest dimensions' as far as Vienna. Here the substitution of a 4–6–4 tank engine caused the traveller some misgivings for its small wheels made him think at first that it was a shunter. But he need not have worried, for 'in spite of our 5-feet 5-inch wheels we scuttled along with the great abandon and arrived at Linz panting for water, to find that we had run 118 miles in 133 minutes, including the long haul through the Wiener Wald.' The engine would have been one of A Lehner's 4–6–4Ts of class 729, introduced in 1931 and much used both on the Arlberg-Orient and the Orient Express when these formations were fairly light.

Electricity took over at Salzburg for the run through the Arlberg Tunnel to the Swiss frontier at Buchs, and on through Switzerland to Basle. An Alsace Pacific worked the train on to Belfort, followed by an Est Mountain. By this time our commentator had moved into a through coach for Boulogne which had joined the cavalcade earlier and noted that at Chaumont it was detached from the rest of the train, which proceeded to Paris. A restaurant

car and brake were added and the Boulogne coach, now part of a miniature train, was worked forward to Laon by an Est 4–6–0. A Nord Pacific completed the journey to the English channel. The whole run of 2200 miles (3540 km) had taken 67 hours, and 17 different types of locomotive had been involved. Such an experience cannot be repeated unless one were to fall asleep over an old *Continental Bradshaw* and dream.

Although Poland put a large electrification program in hand after World War II, by the end of the 1970s it was still operating the largest fleet of steam locomotives in Europe. During the nineteenth century period of railroad development Poland was divided between Prussia, Russia and Austria and its railroad system was operated as parts of the system of those countries. The railroads in the Russian sector were broad gauge, but most were converted to standard gauge during World War I, when the whole country was occupied by Germany and Austria. Today the Polish main line network is wholly standard gauge. The Polish State Railways also operate some local lines of various narrow gauges.

As a result of frontier changes after 1918, East Prussia was separated from the rest of Germany by a strip of Polish territory extending to the Baltic coast. This was the Polish Corridor, a name which became all too familiar in the critical years leading up to 1939. Several railroad routes from Germany to East Prussia traversed it, the most important being the main line from Berlin to Marienburg and Konigsberg which crossed the corridor from Firschau on the west to Dirschau on the east, a distance of about 60 miles (96 km), followed by the short stretch of 11 miles (18 km) to Marienburg which crossed territory belonging to the Free City of Danzig. Through trains between Germany and East Prussia by this route were hauled across the corridor by Polish locomotives, and passengers not holding Polish passports or visas were not allowed to alight. Among the corridor services was the Riga portion of the 'Nord Express.'

The line from Stettin to Dirschau via Gdynia and Danzig entered the corridor at the German frontier station of Gross Boschpol, and trains by this route were worked under arrangements similar to those of the main corridor crossing. Various less important lines were severed completely when the corridor was created, and the situation as a whole was a source of considerable bitterness in Germany.

Because of the history of the country, German and

Above: A JS class 2–8–4 passenger locomotive of the Soviet Union Railways at Voronesh.
Right: Class TKt 2–8–2T No 184 arrives at Nasielsk with the 13.29 from Ilawa on 2 October 1975.
Below right: US-built 2–10–0 Ty246.30 passes Tarnowskie Gory with a coal train on 10 August 1975.

Austrian locomotive designs were numerous in Poland after World War I, some being received as reparations. Certain classes of Polish design were built, and some German designs were developed by the Poles, such as the Polish Ok22 class 4–6–0 based on the Prussian P8 but with a bigger firebox and higher-pitched boiler, giving the class a quite different appearance from the original. One of the most numerous types was the Ty23 class 2–10–0 of which 610 were built from 1923 onwards. In the next decade the more modern Ty37s of the same wheel arrangement were introduced, followed after World War II by the class Ty45 2–10–0s. Also in Poland at this time were large numbers of both German *Kriegslokomotiven* which had been built for Poland during the German occupation, and the British built 2–8–0 'Liberation' locomotives which in Poland were classified Tr202. The United States contributed 2–8–0s and 2–10–0s to ease the postwar motive power shortage, and the Poles built more 2–8–2s developed from the Reichsbahn 19–101 class, and classified Pt47 by the Polish State Railways.

Poland continued to be visited by steam enthusiasts from Western Europe up to the end of the 1970s and at this period it was described as 'without doubt the steamiest country this side of the Bosphorous.' One visitor in 1978 recorded over a thousand steam locomotives of 15 different types seen during a single week.

# 9. The Wider World

The starting point for this last look round the world of steam is the African continent. Here some of the largest steam locomotives in the world worked out their final years. Africa saw the ultimate development of the Beyer-Garratt articulated locomotive, a design developed for countries where increasing traffic had to be worked over lines which had been laid originally with light rails for reasons of economy. The tractive effort that can be usefully developed by a locomotive is limited by the weight on the axles. If the effort exceeds a certain proportion of that weight, adhesion is lost and the wheels slip on the rails. The permanent way restricts the load that can be placed on an axle, and so to haul heavy trains it may be necessary to spread the locomotive weight over a large number of driving axles, each contributing a relatively small proportion of the total tractive effort. In a conventional locomotive this would involve a long rigid wheelbase and consequent difficulties in negotiating curves, particularly the sharp curvature of many lines in the less-developed countries where heavy engineering works were kept to the practicable minimum. Various types of articulated locomotives have been designed for such conditions. One of the

best-known and longest-lasting articulation systems is the Beyer-Garratt, a name associated in particular with very powerful locomotives on narrow-gauge lines in Africa.

The Garratt system of construction was devised by H W Garratt, a British engineer, who patented it in 1908. The manufacturing rights were taken up by the Manchester firm of Beyer Peacock & Co Ltd, so that locomotives built on Garratt's principle are often referred to as Beyer-Garratts. A Beyer-Garratt consists in effect of two bogie-mounted steam engines taking steam from a common boiler which is carried on a cradle slung between them. With no machinery below the boiler itself, the usual constraints on the side of firebox and grate are removed. The 'power' bogies at each end of the machine usually carry guiding as well as driving axles but the overall wheelbase of each is short and the locomotive adapts itself well to severe curvature.

Typical Garratt territory is found in East Africa, where the prewar Kenya and Uganda Railways used the type very extensively on their meter-gauge system. This system began using Garratts in 1926. The permanent way on its main line from Mombasa

Left: A Stanier 2–8–0 of LMS origin works out its years to retirement in Asiatic Turkey, near Ankara.
Right: A German-built 4–6–4T of the Turkish State Railways makes ready to emerge from Haydarpasa shed on the eastern shore of the Bosphorus opposite Istanbul.

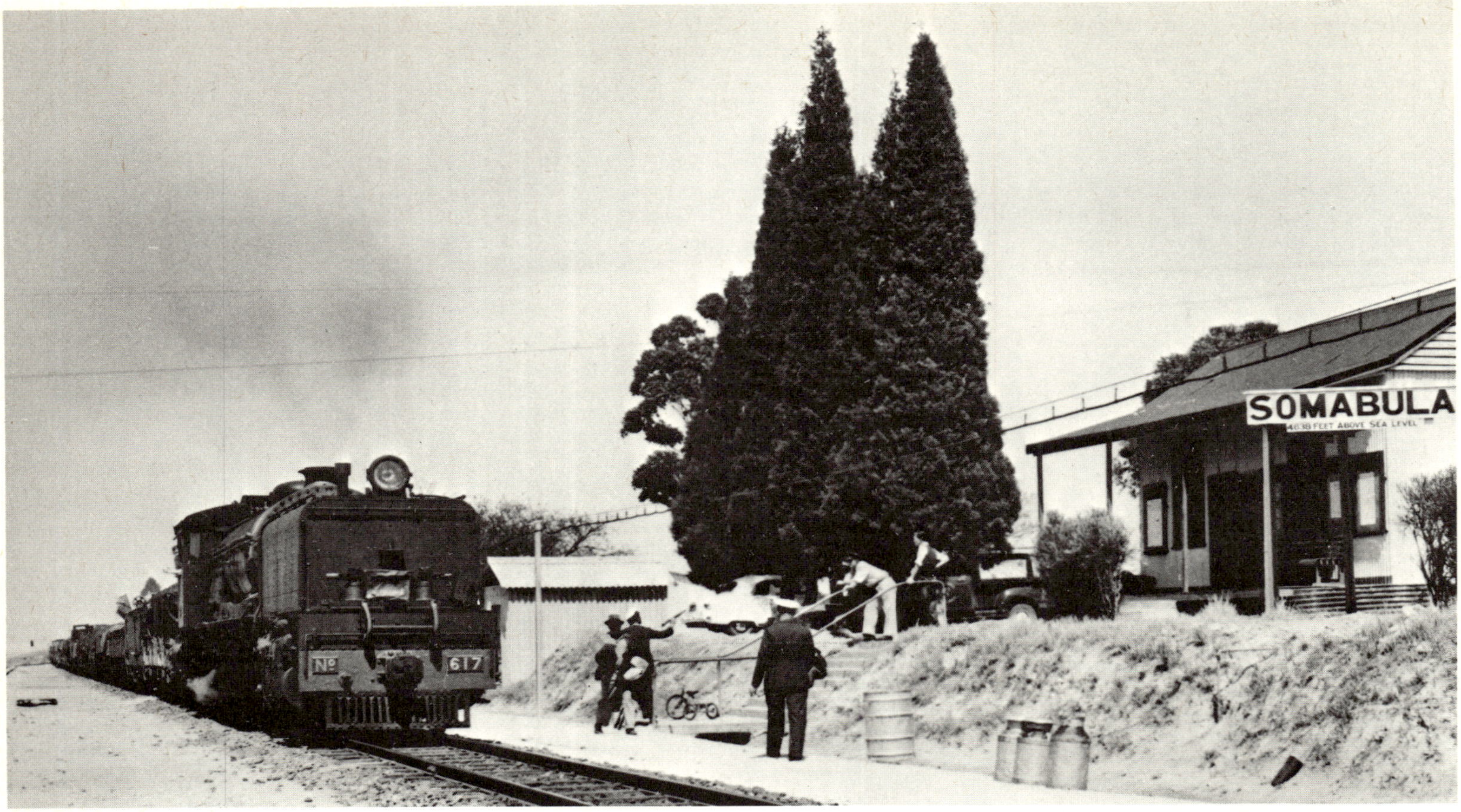
SOMABULA
FEET ABOVE SEA LEVEL
No 617

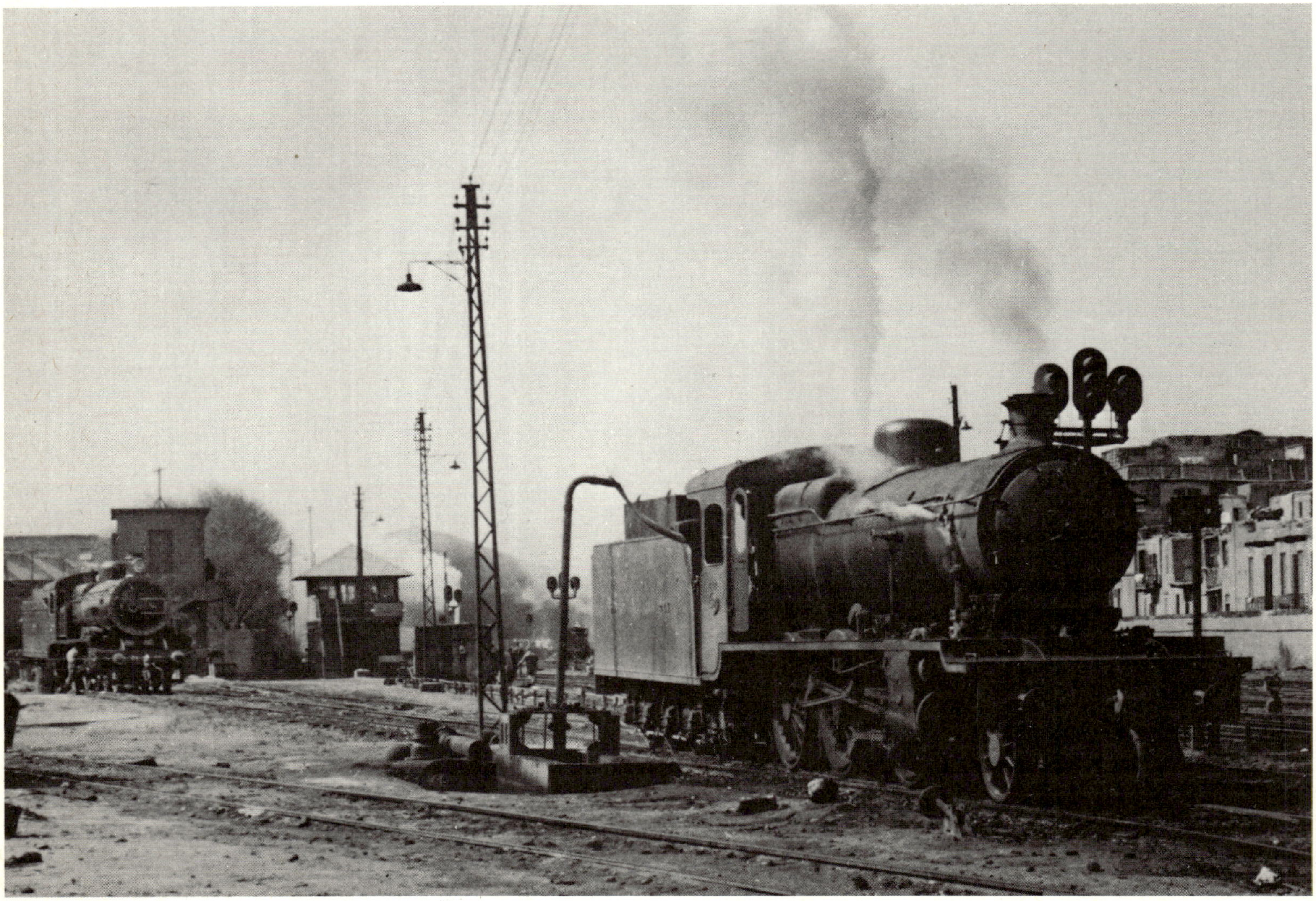

Above: Rhodesia Railways 16A class Garratt (2–6–2+ 2–6–2) at work in 1975.
Above left: A Rhodesia Railways Garratt at Somabula, 4638 feet above sea level, on the main line from Bulawayo to Salisbury.
Left: Egyptian State Railways 2–6–0 No 597 at Cairo Main Shed in 1946. This locomotive was built in 1928 by Armstrong Whitworth.

to Kampala restricted axleloads to 13.16 US tons/ 11.75 UK tons/12 tonnes, but the EC3 class Garratt introduced in 1939 produced a tractive effort of 46,100 lb (20,910 kg). These were the first Garratts with the 4–8–4+ 4–8–4 wheel arrangement and the largest and heaviest engines built up to that time to work over rails weighing only 50 lb (22.7 kg) per yard. They were employed on the section between Nairobi and Kampala, a distance of 550 miles (885.1 km), on which the line climbs to a summit of 9000 feet (2743 m) at Timbora, shortly after crossing the equator, and there are long stretches with a ruling gradient as steep as 1-in-50.

After World War II, when the system merged into the East African Railways, a still larger Garratt was introduced for working between Mombasa and Nairobi, on which heavier rails had by that time been laid, permitting an axle-load of 23 US tons/21 UK tons/21.3 tonnes. This was the class 59 4–8–2+ 2–8–4, weighing 282 US tons/252 UK tons/256

tonnes and developing a tractive effort 83,350 lb (37,807 kg). With these locomotives schedules between Mombasa and Nairobi were accelerated by 33 percent. Train loads up to 1120 US tons/1000 UK tons/1016 tonnes were worked over 1-in-50 gradients and around curvatures so severe that sometimes the driver could see the tail end of his train running parallel with him but in the opposite direction. When the 'Big Boy' Mallets in the United States were withdrawn in the late 1950s, the EAR class 59 Garratts became the world's largest steam locomotives.

On the 3-foot 6-inch (1.067-m) gauge Rhodesia Railways the Garratt locomotive was the principal motive power for both freight and passenger services up to dieselization, and returned to service when oil supplies became difficult. In the final design for this system coupled wheels of 4 feet 9 inches (1448 mm) diameter gave the locomotives a useful turn of speed and 55 mph (88.5 kph) was easily obtained. An

Below left: A South African
Railways 4–8–2+2–8–4
Garratt of class GMAM
pauses at Koloniesplaas
with a Mossel Bay-to-
Johannesburg express.
Below: A 58th class
(4–8–2+2–8–4) Garratt of
the East African Railways
crosses a viaduct near Fort
Ternan on the Kisumu
branch.

observer who has ridden on the footplate of these
locomotives has commented on their very smooth
negotiation of curves at speeds of this order, free
from lurching or oscillation, and considered them an
object lesson in the design of the steam locomotive as
a vehicle. These 15th class locomotives, of 4–6–4+
4–6–4 wheel arrangement, used to work through
between Bulawayo and Mafeking, a distance of 484
miles (778.9 km). Two crews took turns driving and
thus made the round trip of twice that distance. The
engines were hand-fired and worked by a three-man
crew, one man helping with bringing coal forward
from the bunker ready for the fireman, and undertaking other duties. The 15th class locomotives developed a tractive effort of 47,496 lb (21,544 kg).
For still heavier duties, principally freight, on the
Northern main line the 20th class 4–8–2+2–8–4
was introduced, equipped with mechanical stoker
and developing 69,330 lb (31,448 kg) tractive effort.
This class could take loads of 1792–1904 US tons/
1600–1700 UK tons/1626–1727 tonnes over the
severely curved and steeply graded line from
Thompson Junction, Bulawayo, to Victoria Falls on
the border with Zambia, where on one section the
line climbs for 20 miles (32.2 km) at an uninterrupted
1-in-150, curving continuously all the way.

The South African Railways, of the same gauge as

the Rhodesian system, began testing Garratt locomotives as early as 1921 and found them preferable
in South African conditions to the Mallet type of
articulation. Beginning with a modest 2–6–2+
2–6–2, by 1929 the railways were using the massive
GL class 4–8–2+2–8–4 with a tractive effort of
89,130 lb (40,430 kg). For more general service the
GM class of the same wheel arrangement was introduced in 1938. On the 1-in-40 gradients of the line
from Johannesburg to Zeerust the GMs handled
loads of 784–840 US tons/700–750 UK tons/711–
762 tonnes to the same schedules as previous locomotives which had been restricted to 504–560 US
tons/450–500 UK tons/457–508 tonnes. The Garratt
was the type of steam locomotive with the greatest
potential for development in the last days of steam
and might well have exceeded the performance of the
largest actually built.

In conventional locomotives the South African
Railways long favored the 4–8–2 and ultimately
about half of the railways' steam stock was of this
wheel arrangement. Between 1935 and 1939 the
4–8–2 locomotives of classes 15E, 15F and 23 were
reaching the practicable limits of size without a four-
wheel trailing truck to support a larger boiler and
firebox. The next step was to a 4–8–4, ordered in
1951 and delivered between 1953 and 1955.

Above: A preserved class R 4–6–4 of the Victorian Railways heads an enthusiasts' special in 1974.

The 140 4–8–4s ordered were supplied jointly by the German firm of Henschel & Son and the North British Locomotive Co Ltd of Glasgow. Water-supply problems were acute in some areas of South Africa and 90 of the locomotives were therefore equipped with condensing tenders in which condensate from exhaust steam was collected for return to the boiler. The exhaust steam also drove a blower in the smokebox to provide draft for the fire, and five fans in the tender which circulated air over the condensing elements. Overall length of the locomotive and condensing tender was nearly 108 feet (33 m), and the tender was longer than the engine itself. These locomotives could run some 600 to 700 miles (966 to 1126 km) between water stops and travelled at speeds up to 55 mph (89 kph). Water recovery from the steam was of the order of 75 to 78 percent.

In a geographical context, this chapter would be the place in which to mention the steam locomotives of India and Sri Lanka. However, since we are dealing with those countries in which steam has been 'lost,' India and Sri Lanka do not qualify. Happily they are Mecca for enthusiasts who now travel thousands of miles to see genuine steam railroads – as opposed to preserved lines – still at work.

After World War I Turkey was one of several countries to receive examples of the 29 standard German Reichsbahn types. A modified version of the G12 2–10–0 of 1917–24 and many of the G8[2] 2–8–0s were brought in under the reparation scheme but by 1926 the Turkish railway authorities were turning to improvisation on the Prussian P8 4–8–0. This became the 57.001 class 2–10–2, with the same boiler, narrow firebox, and an axle-load of 14.8 US tons/13.2 UK tons/13.4 tonnes. With driving wheels of 4 feet 7.12 inches (1400 mm), the 'new' class worked on light lines.

From Germany to Turkey also went the 46.051 class 2–8–2s and 56.001 class 2–10–0 of 1937 and these two striking types became mainstays of national steam motive power. The former in particular attracted considerable prestige for their passenger traffic working, while the latter carried out stalwart mixed-traffic duties.

The British influence was strong in Egypt both from the fact that the country attracted many Britons to make and run its railways and locomotives but also because the Egyptian State Railway had a distinct preference for the British style of design. In 1926 it took a supply of 4–4–2s and in 1949 4–6–0s were ordered to help replenish the stock of steam motive power after World War II. Immediately after the war Egypt was one of several countries to receive British War Department 2–8–0s and 2–10–0s.

However, they preferred the Stanier 2—8—0 and in 1952 ordered 20 of them from British Vulcan.

France was also well represented in Egypt. In 1905 the Egyptian State chose the de Glehn system in a 4—4—2 with 6-foot 8.5-inch (2045-mm) wheel diameter, 18.9 US-ton/16.9-UK-ton/17.2-tonne axle-load and total weight of 74.4 US tons/66.4 UK tons/67.5 tonnes. French simple expansion was represented by the 4—6—0s of 1952, with 6-foot (1829-mm) wheel diameter, 24.1-US-ton/21.5-UK-ton/21.8-tonne axle-load and all-up weight of 98.3 US tons/87.8 UK tons/88.8 tonnes. There were also the 4—6—2s of 1955 with 6-foot 9-inch (2057-mm) wheels, and total weight of 122 US tons/109 UK tons/110.8 tonnes.

In Victoria, Australia, locomotives were streamlined in 1937 to work the 'Spirit of Progress' express between Melbourne and Albury. In those days there was a break of gauge at Albury on the trans-continental route and travellers from Melbourne or further west for Sydney had to change there. New all-steel coaches were built for the train and four of the S class Pacifics were streamlined and painted blue to work it. Larger tenders were fitted so that they could run the 197 miles (317 km) between Melbourne and Albury without a stop. Average speed from Melbourne to Albury was 49.8 mph (80.1 kph), the train having to climb to a summit of 1145 feet (349 m) above sea level in the first 33.25 miles (53.5 km). Westbound the running was easier and the train averaged 53.3 mph (85.8 kph).

Diesel locomotives replaced the Pacifics in 1952, which were put on fast freight duties. By this time, however, reboilering was becoming necessary if they were to remain in traffic. It was decided to withdraw them, and by 1954 all had been scrapped. Even during this period, however, new steam locomotives were still being taken into service on the Victorian Railways. Deliveries had begun in 1951 of 70 R class 4—6—4s from the North British Locomotive Co Ltd. They were replacements for the A-2 class 4—6—0s, of which 125 had been built in Australia between 1907

and 1915. Up to the arrival of the 4—6—4s they had been working the 'Overland' interstate express among other important duties, and had been brought up-to-date with modernized front ends, large-diameter chimneys and smoke deflectors. But the R class had only a short life span. After running in on fast freight, they were put on crack passenger services, but as more diesels arrived they were soon back on freight and secondary services. One of the class was successfully converted for firing with pulverized coal in 1954 and orders were given for all 70 engines to be fitted similarly, but accelerating diesel deliveries caused the order to be cancelled. Withdrawals began in 1960 after one of the class had been damaged in an accident. Soon all disappeared except two for running enthusiasts' specials.

One of the classic Australian locomotive classes was the C-36 4—6—0 of the New South Wales Government Railways introduced in 1925 as a measure of modernization. At that time passenger loads were increasing and the older P-6 4—6—0s dating from 1892 could only cope with the traffic by double-heading. All 75 of the C-36 class were built in Sydney. They were put on the principal passenger duties and soon earned a reputation as free steamers and fast runners. As late as 1943 some of the crews preferred them to the then-new C-38 Pacifics and they were claimed to have reached 100 mph (161 kph) when making up time. Some remained in service well into the diesel era but in 1968 they were 'blacked' by a railway union because of complaints that they lacked certain modern fitments and their reverse gear was difficult to operate, requiring 19 turns of the wheel from full forward to full reverse. In addition the gear sometimes jammed and had to be freed with a coal pick. A few of the engines were fitted with power reverse and better facilities for the crew but their return to duty was short-lived and all were out of regular traffic by September 1969.

On the freight side, New South Wales moved into the 'big engine' era in 1929 with the D-57 class

Above left: An express from Opua to Auckland is headed by Ja class 4—8—2 No 1284 near Makarau.

**Above:** A J class 4—8—2 pilots a K class 4—8—4 of the New Zealand Government Railways, representing two stages in the development of powerful locomotives for the NZGR which began with the appointment of P R Amgus as CME in 1931.

**Right:** A W class tank heads an Auckland—Papakura train on Parnell Bank.

**Next page:** H class 0—4—2 locomotives prepare for the assult on the Rimatuka incline on the route from Wellington to the Wairarapa Plains, which climbs for 2.5 miles at between 1-in-16 and 1-in-13. These are Fell-system locomotives with additional horizontal driving wheels bearing on on a central third rail.

4–8–2s, which were the most powerful non-articulated locomotives in Australia. Their tractive effort was 67 percent higher than any of the existing NSW freight locomotive classes, most of which were 2–8–0s. The D-57s were three-cylinder engines with the Gresley conjugated drive for the valves of the inside -cylinder, although the design was by the NSW Railways and the whole class was built in Sydney. Power reverse and automatic stokers were fitted.

Although there was an essentially British element Australian locomotives, Australia was introduced to American practice from the early 1920s with such features as hopper ashpans, self-cleaning smoke-boxes, rocking grates and grease lubrication of main bearings. The D-57s, followed by the C-38 Pacifics of 1943, represented the ultimate takeover of American influence which had gathered pace from 1926, when the South Australian Railway had brought in 4–6–2s, 4–8–2s and 2–8–2s which, though built in Britain, were essentially American designs. Even as late as 1953 – three years after the last steam locomotive had been built for an American railroad – the Baldwin-Lima Corporation was building a series of 20 US-designed 2–8–2 freight engines.

Important advances in steam motive power for New Zealand were made in the 1930s under the regime of P R Angus, who became chief mechanical engineer of the Government Railways in 1931. His K class 4–8–4 was considered a masterpiece of design for its tractive effort of 30,815 lb (13,978 kg) with an axle-load of only 16 US tons/14 UK tons/ 14.2 tonnes and for the size of its boiler despite the restricted loading gauge, and the 3-foot 6-inch (1.067-m) rail gauge of the system. Later developments of this design were the Ka class built between 1939 and 1950, incorporating contemporary improvements such as roller bearings and high-tensile steel frames; and the six booster-fitted Kb engines of 1939. These were basically Ka class engines with a booster. In the earlier K class provision had been made for fitting a booster if necessary. It was not required on K class duties in the North Island, but increasing traffic on the Midland line in the South Island led to the decision to build six basically Ka engines with a booster in the trailing truck. Thus equipped, the locomotives had a tractive effort of 36,815 lb (16,700 kg). Progress continued with the 4–8–2s of class J and the oil-fired class Jb, which met the need for a modern express locomotive capable of fast running on light rails, the axle-load being restricted to 12.9 US tons/11.5 UK tons/11.7 tonnes. Forty J class locomotives were built by the North British Locomotive Co Ltd, of which 12 were later converted for oil-firing. As delivered in 1939–40, the locomotives had a streamlined casing and in this form characterized the climax of the express steam locomotive in New Zealand.

New Zealand's most prolific locomotive was the A6 class Pacific, which was used as a maid-of-all-work for many years. Between 1915 and 1926 the NZR had 152 of the class built either in New Zealand or imported from Scotland.

The light axle-loading of the class made it suitable for almost every type of route the country had to offer. In addition, although their driving wheels were only 4 feet 6 inches (1372 mm) they were free running and therefore useful on main-line passenger services until they were superseded by 4–8–2s and 4–8–4s.

189

# INDEX

## Picture credits